TORN

A Tale of Life in the Ozark Mountains

A.B. Poyner

Torn

A.B. Poyner

ISBN (Print Edition): 978-1-66787-609-2

ISBN (eBook Edition): 978-1-66787-610-8

This is a work of fiction. Any resemblance to actual events or persons, living or dead, is entirely coincidental.

To my heart,
My Allen
For believing in me.

In Memory of
MY beloved Nonnie
and
my cheerleader
Kathy Ann Anderson

Special thanks to
Heather and Lucretia

Dedicated to the ones who came before
And the ones who come after.

CONTENTS

FOREWORD

Thoughts from the author...

In every family there are storytellers. Secret keepers. Historians.

They are the ones that sketch the family tree. The ones who honor the graves. The folks who know the saga-who married who, where we all came from. They are the ones who count the costs.

This story was born when I was 8 years old, in my great grandmother's parlor. It was filled with velvet furniture, dust, creepy antique dolls, Avon, and canary cages. I can still smell her musty perfume scent. She drew pictures with words while she spoke of the reservation and her cafe.

Later, in my teens, I scribbled madly in the front seat of an old Scout as my grandfather drove across his farm and spun tales of his depression era childhood and his time overseas during WWII.

I have my grandma's diaries.

I keep a series of notebooks with maps and notes from over 20 years of outings with my mom, grandmother, aunt and great aunt as we honored our ancestors on Decoration Day

If we are lucky enough, there is one in each generation.

A record keeper. A memory hoarder. They remind us of who we are, where we come from, and who we can be.

This time, I guess it's me.

1

Every soul has a path to trod. There are hills and valleys. Some find that you can't go back home again. And we must not forget the tales that are known as generational curses that can tear families apart.

For the young girl it started with a perfectly normal every day walk. Delphi had been up the road to the neighbors to trade some of her mother's butter and eggs for some needles and much desired thread. It worked like that in the Ozark Mountain of Arkansas back in those days. Few people had any real money. Even fewer had enough to put in an actual bank. There was no mercantile in the immediate area. Besides, the closest town was Alpena Pass, and it was at least 12 miles away. So, a little past noon on a sunny June Tuesday, 14-year-old Delphi Little Hawk found herself strolling home on a dirt road. She sang hymns as she went. They were the only songs she knew, as her family had no radio and church was the only social outlet in her rural area. Of course, that was aside from the Tribal Osage and Cherokee prayer chants and songs that she had learned at the knees of her mother. Occasionally, Delphi gave way to impulse and plucked a wildflower or particularly pretty weed that caught her eye.

The hymnals and thoughts of the meeting house were what made her smile when she saw the tall dark man. He was riding towards her on a mule, just up the road. She recognized him from the last few services and singings at the little stone Denver Church. It served the surrounding farms in Carroll County that were out past the town of Alpena Pass. The preaching there did not lean towards any one denomination. Delphi didn't even know about doctrines and dogmas. Just the Bible, plain and simple. And this man had come to their church a few months ago as a travelling preacher. He was Osage, just like her mother and her mother's mother. Her father's people were Cherokee. But since tribes had been gathered up on reservations, if you didn't live with your tribe, most people were just Indians. That is what the white people called them all. Injuns, Indians. It didn't matter. You tried to blend in, and you didn't really have a tribe anymore. This made the old ones sad. But Delphi knew no other way. She knew she was Osage and Cherokee, but truly, she had just been elated to meet a preacher man that was the same color as her. The same blood. A man of God that was not white.

She remembered hearing someone call him Joseph. She lifted a hand to hail him in the accepted manner of a young girl to an elder male.

"Hello Mr. Joseph."

"Delphi Little Hawk," he said as he brought the mule to a halt and tipped his hat,

"Just the young lady I needed to see. I am searching for your father's farm and a neighbor pointed me this way, but I have come to two crossroads and find myself completely lost."

Delphi threw back her head and laughed. How could anyone get lost in such a small settlement? It was in her nature to find light, humor, and joy in every exchange and experience.

"Follow me, Mr. Joseph. I am headed home now."

With little conversation between them, Joseph Tall Chief pulled Delphi up onto the mule's withers and turned back in the direction she indicated. They passed the time chatting about the last sermon and even singing together. But Delphi noticed that Mr. Joseph was becoming more and more quiet. Her questions and comments more terse answers until he was not responding at all. And that is when he turned off the dirt road and headed down a little path towards Long Creek. She began to protest, but his left arm dropped from the reins and tightened around her waist.

After, when she was picking her way back towards the road, she was confused. She knew she had screamed, but she wasn't sure why. No one was around to hear. How would she explain her torn shift to her mother? Or the length of her absence? She didn't even know the words for what had happened to her. And no one would believe her. Mr. Joseph was a man of God. She bent over and wretched the contents of her stomach into the weeds. She could still smell the sweat from his body. Her mouth and jaw were sore and bruised from his silencing hand. And the pain else-where was like nothing she could describe. It was a bad dream. But it was sunny June. And she was not asleep.

When Delphi finally made her way back to the farm, she was relieved to find the house empty, except for her 16-year-old sister Jettimae. Her mother must be out in the fields with the men.

"Delphi! Where have you been? Ma has wanted you for near an hour now. And oh my, what have you been up to? Why are you so...so...torn up? It looks like you've been rolling in a briar patch!"

Delphi felt the tears began to fall. Yes, that is exactly what had happened in a manner of speaking. She tried hard to get the words out and explain to Jetty the devilish prank that had been played. But her nerves overtook her again and she ran back out the door and wretched some more.

By the time the telling was over, Delphi had learned a new word. She had never expected to hear such language from her sister, but liar, imp, troublemaker-all these she knew. Then Jetty had aimed a new word her way: WHORE. Delphi's sister had proclaimed herself judge, jury, and hangman all in one outcry. Jetty had called her a whore. Now she KNEW she could not tell her mother, nor anyone else.

June turned into July and July into August. It was hot and humid just like every year. They toiled in the house and in the gardens just like always. And the only relief was church and the singings. Delphi had been terrified to go at first, afraid to see Mr. Joseph again. But he was not there. He never came again. Everything was just as it had been. Except her courses had stopped. She did not bleed in July, and she did not do so in August. Jetty would not talk to her. She did not treat her meanly in front of family, but she was cold and distant. Delphi knew she had to loosen Jetty's jaws. Only Jetty might know what was going on. And why her courses stopped when that man hurt her.

Had something broken inside?

Jetty was clearing out the last of the bean vines from the vegetable patch when Delphi took her chance. At first, she just knelt and started working beside her older sister. But then, she found her tongue, her courage.

"Jetty, what does that mean? To be a whore?"

Jetty turned her bright red angry face towards Delphi and spat,

"a devil woman. A Magdalene. Jezebel. One who takes what is NOT hers from a man outside of marriage. And Mr. Joseph was coming to court ME. And now you have shamed us all and he has gone away, and I will NOT be married!"

Delphi was speechless. Jetty had made a marriage pact with Mr. Joseph. That horrible thing he did to her was something Jetty would prize. Something to be jealous of? She began to protest. But Jetty shoved her hard and she fell back off her heels onto her bottom. Jetty stood up and started to stomp off.

"Jetty, wait! Please! I don't understand. I didn't want…that. He fought me. And now my courses have stopped, and I think I am…damaged somehow."

"No, whore, you are not damaged. You are ruined. Get ready for a baby, ninny. The baby that should have been mine."

September crept in and Delphi walked through her days like a whisper, like a ghost. She became completely incapable of doing anything more than simply putting one foot in front of the other.

Major changes were coming her way. She could not have fathomed what her future held.

One day after the noon meal, her mother came to her.

"Delphi, I don't know why or how, but I know what you are hiding. And I know you are a good girl. So, I have spoken to Pa, and you must go talk to him now as well. "

Delphi began to shake. She imagined the earth opening to swallow her. She could not face her father. But face him she must. Delphi slowly headed toward the barn. Each step… a mile. Each yard…an eternity. When she entered the building, she was surprised to see not only her father there, but Ramsey Youngblood. He was the young neighbor whose fields butted up to those of the Little Hawk Farm. Mr. Ramsey was always kind, and she knew him from Church. He was white, but he had never looked down on them or failed to shake her father's hand.

Delphi's father stepped in front of Delphi and raised her chin.

"Sweetling, you know Mr. Ramsey."

Delphi silently nodded her head. At that, Mr. Ramsey began to speak. His voice was soft and kind and deep.

"Delphi, that travelling preacher is gone. He will never come back. And if he does, your Pa and I...well, your Pa and I will make sure he never hurts you or anyone else again. But that doesn't quite fix the mess he has made for you, does it?"

Delphi looked from one man to the other, her mouth open in despair and mortification. Mr. Ramsey looked at Delphi's father, who nodded, then Ramsey took a step forward and put his hand in Delphi's.

"Your Pa and I are real good friends. And good neighbors. You know I lost my wife, Annie, last year to pneumonia. And you know I am left with two boys. Nine and six. Boys turn into trouble without a mother around. And ladies with a baby and no husband, well they get left in a mess too. Delphi, I talked to your Pa, and if you marry me, I will never hurt you and you and your baby will be my family along with Ramy and Little Joe, my sons. Your folks will just be across the field and your mama will be right on hand to help you learn to be a wife and mother. I will love you and be grateful if you would help me fill my house with laughter again."

Ramsey looked so humble. He didn't care that she was Osage, or that her baby was not his. His eyes were kind and warm. She believed him. And she believed God. God had a care for even the tiniest sparrow. And oh, how she had prayed since June that God would send her Boaz as he had sent to Ruth in the Bible.

"Pa?" Just the single word. She was a good girl, and she trusted her father. Pa shook his head yes.

"Sunday after next, right after the singing. I'll ride over to the Preacher Thomas today. It's the right thing Delphi. Ramsey is a good God-fearing man."

Ramsey tilted her head up and gave her a kiss on the cheek. As soft and sweet as the rain in Spring.

She left them then, her father and the man who would be her husband, standing in the barn talking and making plans. She made her way slowly across the yard, her head closer to the clouds than her feet were to the grass. She was thinking about what it would be like to have her own kitchen and two little boys. For the first time since her new circumstances had occurred, she let herself think of the baby. Her baby. Their baby. She knew Ramsey was a good daddy. Ramy and little Joe were good, happy boys. And they were even CLEAN on Sundays. Maybe God would send them a baby girl. Esther.... she loved that story in the Bible. Esther saved her people. Maybe she would name her little girl Esther.

She didn't worry or bother with thoughts about leaving home. Her whole life her mother had raised her to grow up and run a house, be a God-fearing obedient wife, and a good mother who would teach her children the Bible, and how to read and how to grow up and raise the next generation. Delphi was pondering her NEW home and what she would need to take with her into her marriage. Suddenly she stopped and dropped to her knees right there by the lilac bush. She spoke out loud in the Spirit as she prayed to God and counted off her blessings. She gave her thanks and worshipped the Lord's ability to make beauty from ashes.

Delphi was too busy speaking to God to notice Jetty watching her from the corner of the house. Her face was tilted to the heavens, so she did not see Jetty spit in her direction and stomp off out of sight.

Delphi and her mother were cooking supper and discussing the basics that should always be kept in the larder. How to make dough rise for bread. How long milk and butter would keep in a spring house. A few days ago, Ma, Pa, and Delphi had taken the wagon over to Ramsey's and moved most of Delphi's things into his house. She didn't have much. And his house was nice sized compared to the Little Hawks' over full clapboard. She adored the little boys, and they were jumping and tumbling over each other and everyone else trying to help "Little Mama" move things. Delphi and her mother had also spent every spare moment talking about childbirth and man/wife love, as her mother called it, while they sewed new drawers and shifts and two new dresses for Delphi. One was the most beautiful yellow fancy church dress Delphi had ever seen. The other was a calico for better if not best. Her current clothes would all become everyday clothes except her church dress. It would join the new calico as "second best" and the yellow would be her wedding dress, and then serve for the most special occasions. Pa had taken her to Alpena Pass and bought her a new pair of shoes and was working on a cradle out in the barn. It was supposed to be a secret, but Delphi knew.

Jetty would help with nothing. Not even when directed by her mother. She simply stayed out of sight all the time. At lunch one day, Ox, Delphi's oldest brother said,

"I reckon Delphi's 'bout married off and Jetty's plumb run away. No girls to keep Ma company."

His father gave him a telling look and lunch continued in silence. Ox and David, the two Little Hawk sons were carrying on with the farm work while Pa was helping Ramsey ready things over at the Youngblood place. They were good brothers and good men. They likely knew more about the situation even than Delphi did, but they knew their sister and they were raised right. And they welcomed the fore coming situation of a new brother-in-law with adjoining acreage and shared work.

Once again, Jetty was not home for this lunch and would not receive a tongue lashing when she DID show up. The first few times Ma and Pa had tried to speak with her about her unladylike and unacceptable manners, she had simply stared them dead in the eye, and said,

"I suppose the splinter in my eye is larger than the post in your other girl's."

Jetty was at an age where she was practically considered an adult, and the situation was delicate. Her parents had talked to no one about it but preacher Thomas. And those were private conversations that mainly involved prayer.

Finally, the night came when Jetty did not come home. Everyone was frantic, but no one was truly surprised. Ox, David, Pa, and Ramsey went on mule and horseback in different directions looking and rounding up men for the search. Ma and Delphi spent the night on their knees in the bedroom praying and waiting. By morning the whole county knew to be on the watch and Ramsey offered to head to Alpena Pass to see if anyone in town had word.

Two days passed and Jetty was on everyone's hearts, in their heads, and unfortunately making rounds in the gossip circles. Ramsey didn't come back for two days. He wouldn't have returned until he had made all the rounds. Jetty was his family now too.

Delphi couldn't help but be afraid that Jetty had done something terrible to get back at her. Something she couldn't even imagine, but something that might take her future with Ramsey away from her. Delphi and Ramsey were never alone together, but they were keeping company and working together as the wedding day was approaching quickly. They had moved past awkward on to shy and now were learning to know each other. Delphi cared for him and felt proud to be his would-be-wife. Many a woman deserved more and got less.

FINALLY, his horse made its dusty trail up their path. He wasn't coming quickly and soon enough he came closer, and they could see he was alone. The only possible thing he could have found would be news. One by one, all the Little Hawks gathered in front of the barn and waited as he approached, dismounted and went to take care of his horse. Ox took the reins and shouldered that task so Ramsey could report to Ma and Pa.

Hat in hand, face towards the ground, Ramsey opened his mouth and shut it again. He chewed on his words a little and then put his hand on Pa's shoulder.

"Atsadi, Neosha," he said, using Pa and Ma's given names, "she has been seen. She is thought to be safe."

Ramsey took his hand off Pa's shoulder and reached out his hand to Delphi. The look on his face was protective and sorrowful and angry all at the same time. Delphi took his hand, and as he pulled her to his side, she suddenly became very afraid. There was a sense of dread that made her want to wretch like she had when the baby first began in her stomach.

Ramsey's next words were slow and level, while he held Delphi beside him in a protective and strong grasp. They had not touched like this before. And she was somewhat comforted.

"Mr. Joseph was seen in town three days ago. He did not leave town or come this way…"

Ramsey said something else, but Delphi did not process it. Much to her horror, she began to feel faint. Right there in front of the whole family and her fiancé. David immediately turned and ran to the house coming back with a wet rag. Ma took it and washed Delphi's face and then folded it and placed it on the back of Delphi's neck. Ramsey never let go of her hand.

Pa put his hand on Ma's back and suggested they move to the porch. Delphi obviously needed to sit, and Ma, if not the men, knew that this kind of shock could loosen the babe and Delphi could slip her child. Ramsey sat beside Delphi and put his arm around her and spoke the most important words next.

"He was only in town two days, and it was last week. He spoke to almost no one. He said nothing about your family that anyone can recall. And now he is gone."

Ramsey looked directly into Delphi's eyes,

"You are safe, and you are the mother of MY child. Everyone knows you are about to be Mrs. Youngblood. However, the day Jetty went missing, they were both seen headed North out of town on Mr. Joseph's mule."

2

The very simple wedding had been the most exciting day of young Delphi's life so far. And goodness knew, her life had been full of changes, twists and turns most recently. Ma had let her have the first bath the night before and poured milk and rose water into the wash tub. It made Delphi's skin soft, and shimmery, and she smelled so good. Ma also rinsed her hair in rose water and then they both sat on the porch and watched the sun go down as Ma combed and combed Delphi's hair for what seemed like hours. Then she began to plait it in intricate braids. Special for the wedding.

They had not said much, just enjoyed this last time of many, many such nights where once all THREE Little Hawk women had sat and braided each other's long shiny black hair.

Then Ma began to speak.

"I knew you were inside me almost as soon as you took root. Your Pa knew you would be a girl. I don't know what signs he read, or what nature or the Creator showed him. But Atsadi knew. You were always quiet and thoughtful. So still and observant. You did not kick much. And when you came, well Delphi, I really don't remember you ever crying. You were my watcher. My Oak Tree. You just took up your place and watched and listened and never were a bit of trouble. You are named after your father's grandma because when you were born, you looked like a tiny version of her. All wrinkled and quiet, with deep still black eyes, wide open all the time. We never knew what she was thinking, and you are the same way."

Delphi turned then and looked at Ma over her shoulder.

"Lots of times Ma, it is better to just BE, instead of pondering. Most questions answer themselves if you watch and listen to everything going on around. And if there is still a question, then I listen harder, so I can hear God."

Ma took Delphi into her arms and with a choking voice said,

"Yes Delphi, and that is why you are going to be just fine."

The next day after services in the church house, Delphi, Ramsey, and their families moved to the front of the room and stood before Preacher Thomas. Ramsey took Delphi's hands and looked into her eyes. She noticed that he had on a new shirt and a right smart bow tied at his neck. Ramy and Little Joe danced around, but they were quiet and trying hard to be still. She grinned down at both of them. They had taken to calling her Little Mama, and that suited her fine. She was barely a head taller than Ramy.

She and her new husband said the words. Everyone bowed their heads and prayed. Ma wiped away a tear and Pa shook Ramsey's hand. David and Ox followed Atsadi's example.

They all headed back to the Little Hawk farm for a luncheon, even Preacher Thomas and his wife and daughter. Only this time, Delphi rode up front on the driver's seat with Ramsey. He lifted her up into the wagon and grinned at her as he made sure the boys were sitting firm on their bottoms in the wagon box.

Then he crossed to the other side, jumped up and took the reins in one hand. With the other, he reached over and took Delphi's hand. This was the first time they had ever been alone without her parents. She looked up at him through lowered eyelashes and gave a small shy smile.

"Delphi, you look right pretty all the time, but in that new dress, well, you look like a daisy, or a jonquil. And your hair is like the night. I sure am proud. Are you tired? Does the baby kick yet?" Ramsey asked with a slight blush.

She couldn't quite look at him, but she spoke up clearly and directly. She wanted this man to see her as a friend, and a partner, and as his Eve. Not as a ruined child.

"Thank you, Ramsey. Ma and I thought that this was a grand color for the time of year. I surely thank you for the compliment."

"And the babe?" he asked. Smiling broader with no blush this time.

Delphi looked him square in the face and scooted an inch closer to him on the seat.

"Mostly I just get tired at night. And I don't feel any kicking right yet. But sometimes it is like I swallowed a moth, or a tiny beating heart. Ma said that is how it starts. That means she's growing, and the kicking will start as she gets stronger."

Ramsey paused,

"She?"

"Yes, sir, husband. I believe you are having a daughter. And I believe God wants her to be called Esther. The People know these things. God tells us with signs and the wind. My Pa knew I would be a girl."

"Well, then, sweetheart, I believe we best start you a list for the next trip to town. My little Esther will need pink ribbons and yarn and fabric. Plenty to keep you busy readying to welcome our little Miss."

Delphi turned in her seat to look at her sons. Ramy and Little Joe were watching for birds and spitting over the side of the wagon. Somehow dirty even though they had barely touched the ground. Her grin split her face ear to ear as she looked overhead at a red tail hawk and whispered a silent prayer of thanksgiving.

The first day of her life as Mrs. Youngblood was mainly spent walking around the farm and house with Ramsey, who she proudly took to calling "Husband" most of the time, which he would return with "Sweetheart."

In the 1890s, it was customary for newlyweds to take a fort-night honeymoon, although most folks could not afford to travel. Family would care for any children from previous marriages and leave the happy couple to their own devices. So Ramy and Little Joe were packed off the Little Hawk farm to be spoiled rotten.

Ramsey showed off the vegetable garden which she took great interest in as this had been one of her primary joys and responsibilities at home growing up. She was also greatly pleased with the size and look of his…. THEIR…. chicken flock. Though she did ask if he would consider adding dominiquers, as they were good regular layers and productive watchful mothers. She directly declared responsibility of the flock as well.

She had not realized the size of his hayfield, nor the num-ber of cattle. There were a few milkers, but the bulk of the herd was beef cattle. He also grew almost 20 acres of corn and had 5 acres in peach trees. This was where his spending money came from. There was more than enough to feed the family, and also to sell in town for profit. Bartering butter, canned peaches, and eggs would also aid in obtaining the things they did not produce. Beef and hay could be traded for pork. And he lived no further from the creek than the Little Hawks did, so fish was a welcome treat on occasion.

Even at fourteen, almost 15, Delphi knew how all this cast a bright future. Her parents not only had included her in their living but relied on her as a working part of the process.

Delphi had grudgingly gotten used to Jetty's absence, so the first few nights, sharing a space with her husband was a little awkward, but quickly she warmed to his presence and slept more soundly than she had since Jetty disappeared. Ramsey was a good Christian man, understanding of what she had experienced, and expected none too much of her in her pregnancy and youth. Truly, he was almost too good to believe. Yet he told her the same thing about herself regularly. Especially after he tasted her cooking.

On Saturday after the first week as a married couple, Delphi dressed in her next best dress, Ramsey donned his good straw hat and tied a ribbon bow at his collar and curried the fine gray horses until they gleamed. Then they headed into town. Alpena Pass. The trip into town for Delphi after the confusing, catastrophic summer and Jetty's disappearance made her nervous. She wasn't showing her condition much yet, but she was aware of gossip and judgement. Ramsey held her hand the entire time.

Their first stop was at the General Store on Carrolton and Main. Indeed, just like he promised, they purchased the softest pink yarn, some equally beautiful yellow, along with ribbon in complimentary colors. Then they went to the fabric. Ramsey encouraged her to choose muslin and 3 different lengths of cotton for tiny gowns and shifts. When they got to the counter, Ramsey shook the merchant's hand and introduced Delphi as his wife to Mr. Smith. Ramsey assured him that anything Delphi needed, whether he was present or not was to be put against the Youngblood account, and likewise, should Delphi come in with butter, eggs, or anything else Mr. Smith was interested in, now came from the Youngblood farm and should be credited to that account. Delphi felt proud and as though she truly belonged with Ramsey now, partners even in the sight of the town.

They then went to the town's hotel and into the restaurant there in the lobby on the ground floor. Delphi had never in her life been in such a place, nor had a stranger wait on her and clean up after a meal. She had Ramsey order her a cup of chamomile tea, which Ma said was calming for the baby. She also chose something called chicken salad. It came on a slice of toast cut horizontally. She chewed and tasted it very slowly.

"Sweetheart, do you like it? Is your meal alright?" Ramsey asked with a worrisome look on his face.

Delphi looked at him with intense and thoughtful eyes,

"Yes, Husband. It is very tasty. I am trying to learn the makings so I can serve it at home."

This earned her a laugh from her husband that started deep in his belly and rolled up and out loud, crinkling his eyes until they almost shut. It was a pleasing sound and made her smile and laugh too.

"What a clever, clever wife I have won."

That night, as they went to sleep after an evening of chores and a simple dinner, Delphi cuddled close to her husband, his hand on her stomach. She slept like a rock.

The Youngbloods were settling in nicely. Delphi enjoyed being "Little Mama" to Ramy and Little Joe.

They were good, smart, sweet little boys. At 9, Ramy was gangly and going to be tall like his father. He was very responsible, if a bit quiet, and a good hand helping on the farm. He was especially good with animals. He sat close to the front of the class in school and already had a head for the Gospels and could sing most any hymn. Often, his voice could be heard matching Delphi's as they went about chores in the afternoons.

Little Joe, at just 6, worshipped the ground his brother walked on. It was not the only reason both Little Mama and Pa were happy that God had blessed them with such a good set of boys. Little Joe was reading and liked to sound out the lines in the newspaper and in the Bible around the kitchen table at night. He couldn't wait until he was a big brother and could help more, like Ramy. But he was still ALL boy. Delphi learned quickly to check pockets before doing the wash and to brace herself for the treasures that tiny boys liked to gather. A worm was not an unusual find.

As Christmas crept upon them, Delphi's tummy grew rounder, Ramsey's smile grew broader, and the boys' excitement was tangible. Delphi had taken to spending Thursdays with her mother and her cooking skills were broadening rapidly. She had, by now, gotten the cold chicken salad down pat. She was also turning out fluffy biscuits and fine sausage gravy. Either of these made an easily served supper on her Thursdays so her boys didn't have to wait or suffer the pains of her absences.

Ramsey was bursting with pride at his little family. When Annie died, he had mourned grievously. They had been sweethearts since grammar school, and married at 16, not at all unusual for their little area. She had been fair and had small bright blue eyes. She was a wonderful mama, and it was almost more than he could bear when she passed away. But his new bride had healed his heart.

There was nothing in either of them that put the other in his mind. Delphi had huge, deep dark eyes. Her hair was her pride, the pride of her People. It was dark as midnight and fell below her hips. She usually wore it in a single, knotted braid at the nape of her neck, but there was no end to the beautiful and extraordinary plaits and styles she would manage on Sundays or trips to town or singings.

Today she had chosen a special waved and braided styling that left half her hair hanging long and dark down her back, all the better for Ramsey to brush aside with his hand. She and her mother had let out her dresses and she wore a nice simple blue today, with a full apron over her growing middle. The boys were with them in the wagon as they made their way to town. They needed some lumber, so Ramsey could finish a few Christmas surprises. Delphi had eggs and butter to trade at the store for a few items and they needed the mail.

Afterwards, they would swing by the Little Hawk farm to share any news and a meal before heading home to evening chores.

Ramsey took the boys with him to the lumber mill after helping Delphi down onto the sidewalk at the General Store. She made her way inside and spoke briefly to the shopkeeper. They had a very good relationship after these several months. He always appreciated the size of her eggs, many double yolkers, and the even color and flavor of her butter. She chose the small trinkets for Ma, Pa, David, and Ox that were on her list for the upcoming holiday, and then went next door to collect the newspaper and mail.

There was a letter postmarked Kentucky. It was from Jetty.

Delphi was still and quiet in the wagon on the trip back to her folk's house. She wasn't sure just how she felt once she had seen the letter sent by Jetty. She did not get sick, but she felt like she might. She saw that it was addressed to Ma. She was glad to know that Jetty must be well enough to write.

Ramsey reached over and laid his large hand on Delphi's small dark one. The look on her face told him that something was not right. She was a calm, quiet little woman, but this was an overwhelmingly silent trip. He tried to guess what she was thinking but fell short. He could only hope that she would soon share her mind.

Once they arrived at the Little Hawk farm, it was only a matter of moments until the entire family was gathered on the front porch greeting one another. Delphi waited for a pause in conversation and then very solemnly handed the unopened letter to her mother. Ma gave her a questioning look, and then gazed down at the folded, marked letter.

"Jetty?" Ma said. "My word...."

November 28, 1898

Wingo Depot, Kentucky

Dear Ma,

I reckon by now you must know that I am to be a wife. Brother Joseph Tall Chief means to marry me and then travel to his family home so he can find work as preaching does not earn a good wage when you are traveling. By now we have crossed over the wide Mississip River and gone quite a piece. Please tell Pa that it is ever so big as he told when giving his story of moving to Arkansas.

I believe you must be confused about me leaving and all the things that Delphi will have had to say about me and Joseph. Having asked me to marry, he told me the whole truth. He did not give her that baby. He often saw her walking the road and says she must have a boy near Denver. It made me grieve to think that she would tell tales on Joseph that way. I do hope that she has stopped all her evil works.

Pray that soon after our wedding, I will have a grandchild for you. And it will be one of a Holy union. If fates will it, maybe we will see you sometime next year when we travel to the reservation in Oklahoma.

Do not worry for me, as to be traveling unaccompanied with Joseph. He said to say we are already married in God's eyes and that the Creator sees no sin there. But we will still seek a licensed marriage once we are settled. Then I can be known as Mrs. Tall Chief. Oh, that will be a happy day.

Give my love to Pa and the boys and know that I am sorry that our family cannot all be together. Joseph says that we cannot raise children around the shame of my sister. But do know that we are praying about Delphi all the time. Joseph says that temptation lays its feet at the simple. I will also pray that you and Pa can forgive her and help her best ways you can.

I must end soon for we are catching a train on the New Orleans and Ohio line to reach the Tall Chief homestead. And I want to end on a happy tick. I have found a good man and a good life, and I will see you all again one day soon, God willing.

Lovingly,

Jettimae

Ma let her hand drop, and the letter with it.

"Stupid, selfish girl. Blind, hateful girl. Oh, my poor Jetty! She does not see the trap he leads for her."

Pa twisted his hat in his hands.

Delphi grabbed the porch railing as everything went dark.

Delphi slowly came back to herself. Ma said women in the family way faint some. Now Delphi sat on the porch and looked sadly at Ramsey and her parents.

"I'll come across that man one day," said Pa.

"Not if he's lucky," Ramsey noted.

Ma had big unshed tears in her eyes. How could Jetty be so thick and love-lost? She had raised her girls up the same and taught them the same values. One was tripped but had fallen softly, and the other was gone, on the whispers of the same bad end. This was absolutely no good whatsoever.

Delphi leaned over and put her head between her knees. She was feeling peaky again. Ramsey brought her some water as David and Ox were sent to the icehouse and for the doctor, respectively. With her youth and the baby at such a delicate stage everyone was concerned for Delphi's health and the baby.

She raised her hand and took the cup of water that Ramsey had brought.

"I reckon some fellas are just bad all the way through, "she whispered, "but he had us all fooled and Jetty now most of all. I am not mad at her, but FOR her. Because when she realizes her state and his dishonesty, she will be in a very bad bind. Mostly we just better pray. Ma, is there any address?"

"Just the Kentucky Depot. We haven't any family left out that way, and they have probably already headed for his home. No, child, I think you're correct. Mostly we just better pray."

Delphi went quietly with her mother and laid down on the bed in the little bedroom that had belonged to the two girls. She looked about her. There were still two of Jetty's older everyday dresses on the pegs. And a sun bonnet. Jetty's doll was gone. It's companion, given to Delphi on her 5th birthday, was waiting back at the Youngblood home in the corner on a chair. Jetty had taken her good shoes and a hair comb with her. And her Bible was also missing. At least Jetty had her Bible. The family records were marked carefully in the front, the way they had seen their father mark the family Bible. Maybe Jetty would remember them when she prayed. Maybe the Bible would bring the family to Jetty's mind if her adventure came to a bad end.

As she sat there thinking, Delphi couldn't help but remember the bad smell on that preacher man. And the way he sang and talked with her and then went silent. And just how Jetty had reacted when asked for help. This was not something that just happened. That man had worked on her sister's mind for a time, Delphi was sure.

Later, when the doctor had come and gone, Ramsey took Delphi carefully home. He put her to bed like the doctor had said. This baby was good sized for its time and might come sooner if she wasn't careful. So, they had to bide their time and make some adjustments.

Ma took to cooking for all of them and Pa or David or Ox would bring over the food for the Youngblood family. Ramy took up some of the minor housework each morning after he milked the cows. Ma came every other day and helped Delphi to new clothes and a wash. Then it was straight back to bed.

The days were long, and Delphi was glad she had her Christmas present projects to keep her busy. She had crocheted a new hat for each person in the family. She had wrapped Jetty's and laid it aside, but the others would all be needed. She carefully worked delicate little flowers to sew onto the cap meant for her mother. Delphi's heart pained her for Ma. She could not imagine the loss of a child. And Ma had taught them so much about how to pray and cook and work. Ma had modeled them both with her very own hands and it was a sore and sorry thing that had happened.

When Delphi took a break from the lavender and green of the flowers for her mother's cap, she worked out four tiny ones in different colors much lighter and fair for a baby. The little socks were done. You could never have enough of those. And there were blankets that needed the edging.

She took it in turns, reading, praying, and singing in the winter sunshine that cast through the window onto her bed. Yes, there was plenty to keep Delphi busy as she waited out the hours to meet her child.

Delphi woke to bright crisp sunshine on Christmas morning. She was excited but also a bit nervous. Later that day, the family would be coming over and Ma was to cook dinner there at the Youngblood home. Ramsey was going to help her down and set her in the rocking chair, so she could enjoy the holiday. But what if the excitement and movement upset the baby? Delphi knew that her daughter needed to stay put for three more months.

She sat up in bed and reached for the wash basin and cloth set up on the little vanity table that her husband had pulled close to the bed. She dabbed the sleep from her eyes and gazed out the window. The air looked like it was ready for snow. When it came to these parts, here in the Ozarks, it could certainly bury a lot in its downy.

Delphi wanted to bury some things. Her sorrow and mourning. Her nervousness and fears. A past of quiet deference to a sister she would never understand. But mostly the heavy ache in her heart that reminded her that her sister was not here. And it also beat out a tempo that told her she meant nothing to Delphi even though her sister meant the world to her. She wondered if she had ever known her at all…

They were out in the garden, looking for lady bugs. Delphi must have been about 7 years old.

"Sissy," she said to Jetty. Her older sister raised an eyebrow but did not stop her examination of the leaves that might hide her prey.

"Sissy, will I be pretty like you when I grow up?"

"Not SO pretty, mayhaps, Bean. You are smaller and darker. But you will be good enough."

They both collapsed into giggles…

Delphi now wondered at the tone and meaning of her sister's words. Jetty hadn't been teasing. Could a rivalry really go back this far? Farther than that? Could Jetty have felt this way for even longer?

Delphi shook her head and chased the thought away. It would not do for a crisp biting Christmas morning. Instead, she gazed at the peak of the mountain just visible out the window. She dreamed of her daughter instead. A daughter that would have two older brothers to love and adore her. And maybe there would be another child in a few years.

Later that morning after Ramsey had set her chair by the fire, she watched Ramy open his ball and bat. He was almost as tall as she was now. And such a good boy. Beyond his impeccable obedience, he worked hard and tried to find things he could do for Delphi. She always thanked him and patted him on the shoulder calling him "young man." He was eager to be helpful and a life saver at times. Little Joe was a good boy too. Ramsey had made him a little wooden train engine. Whenever they went into town, Joe was so excited to see the trains rumble through Alpena Pass. He liked to count the cars and Delphi missed those trips very much now that she was on bedrest and the weather was harsher. Next spring, she would count cars with her little boy again. She could only pray that her new baby was as bright eyed and smart as Joe Joe.

Their stockings were filled with hard candy and bouncing balls. There was a small bag of marbles in each bright green sock. Harvest had been good this year and before she got sickish, Delphi had also canned quite a bit for the family. These small treats were very welcome and the signs of an abundant growing season. God was blessing their union and it was good to see the children so happy.

Ramsey had unwrapped his new leather wallet from the brown paper very carefully. Delphi had saved her butter and egg money and had chosen it special. It was a deep brown calf skin with a pocket and a money clip. She had been so proud when she made the purchase. It was a secret, but she had almost bubbled over with her excitement. She knew her husband would use it and admire it every time he did. She had been so glad to have this gift already before the doctor ordered her to bed.

For his new bride, Ramsey had chosen a beautiful string of beads. They were glass and all the colors of a stream-blue, green, and golden. It was a warm thoughtful gift and Delphi held them up to the sunlight and watched the colors dance. She then looped them around her neck. They were the perfect touch for gaiety on Christmas Day. She knew her Ma would admire them.

A light snow had just started to fall as her parents and the boys arrived. The boys rode the mules and Ma, and Pa were in the wagon. Delphi heard them as they came up on the porch with hugs and greetings for the boys and their son in law. Ma was first through the door, with two packages and a pie. She set these on the table and came straight to Delphi. Kneeling down, she put one hand on Delphi's stomach and the other over Delphi's heart. Neosha quietly listened and concentrated. Then she said a prayer in her soft voice.

"Not today, my girl. All is well."

Delphi was grateful to her mother and knew that her words rang true. Her people were in harmony with the earth and with life and saw the ways all things are connected. The baby gave three fluttering but very distinctive kicks. The women exchanged smiles.

The adults traded gifts. Everyone loved the hats Delphi had made. Likewise, she had socks for the men and a beautifully intricate shawl she had labored over for her mother. It was a Prayer Shawl pattern and worked in the loveliest shade of red. Ma and Pa pulled out the gift they had for their daughter and her husband. It was wrapped in an old quilt – safe for the ride over. Pa had worked late in the evenings, and it showed. Delphi's heart grew big as he unwrapped a handmade oak cradle. Ramsey shook Pa's hand and complimented him on the scrolling along the edges. It was the best present they could have gotten.

After the gifts were opened and everything was properly put away, Ma started working on the ham she had brought from home. Then she rolled out biscuits as Delphi read aloud and watched out the window at the boys and menfolk throwing snowballs.

She had a tiny ache in her throat as she thought, "this is the best day I have ever had."

January was cold and snowy. Delphi was not one for low spirits, but trapped there in the bed, day in and day out...

It was not easy to keep a smile on her face. When her thoughts dragged especially low, she would have a game of checkers with the boys, or work on her nine-patch quilt for the baby. It was going to be lovely. Her ma had brought her some squares of familiar fabric. Here was the dress she wore on her first day of school. And just there, that was the Easter dress that matched one for Ma and one for Jetty. There were several beautiful calicos and other patterns in feminine tones that brought together a slew of memories. That could always perk an afternoon up.

Joe's reading was coming along splendidly. The boys only went to school in spring, since weather and the farm kept them busy the rest of the time. Between what Delphi did at home, and church, they were good pupils and read better than most. On especially cold days, Little Joe would stay inside and read to her out of the Bible or the children's mission books that were distributed by the church.

She truly missed the singings, and since she had mentioned this to Ramsey, every few weeks the whole family would gather at the house and join in on every hymn they could remember. Delphi was touched to know that her people were happy for her and loved her enough to brighten her resting time.

But she became low when she thought of Jetty. Was Jetty thinking of them? Where was she? Married yet? Could she be feeling kicks in her belly soon? Why had that man been able to lie so convincingly to her sister when he was so evil? Why had something not given him away yet? Or HAD he been revealed, and maybe Jetty could not get away?

These thoughts would pervade and that is when Delphi had to stop herself and move on to something positive. For that possibility was too horrible to imagine. She often had dreams that Jetty was home again, and all was well. She took this as good hope.

Now the cradle her pa had made sat in the corner of the room. The beautiful lacy pink blanket Delphi had crocheted draped over the end and a hat and booties were resting inside. She worked diligently on the tiny stiches of the gauzy cotton gowns. March. Her daughter would arrive in March, just as the buds and baby animals. Just 8 more weeks. Not long now until the danger had passed. It had been frightening, but the baby was staying put just as she should. She kicked and turned like no tomorrow, but the doctor said this was an excellent sign. He reminded Delphi when he came that the baby was measuring up to be good sized for such a small young mother and not to worry too much. Worrying and negative thoughts might bring her too soon. No stress. And everyone was pulling together to see to it.

The ground was softer, and a few Easter lilies were creeping thru the frosty dirt. Their yellow heads were a welcome sight amidst the barren winter landscape. Esther would be with Delphi in 6 weeks. Delphi was going to have a little girl and be a mother in her own right. Though that hardly seemed fair, as Little Joe and Ramy had transformed her heart the moment she took them on. She loved being 'Little Mama', and they truly loved her as well. She had tried so hard to give them what they needed and do their true mama, Annie, proud. It was a serious thing to raise another woman's children, and Delphi looked upon it as a calling from God. The gift of her daughter would be like icing on a cake.

Ramsey grew ever more attentive as Delphi's stomach broadened. Between her husband and Ma, there was little she had to do for herself, and Delphi roughened in the chases. She was not good at being helpless. She was used to being sturdy and steady and giving the help, not taking it. However, she tried to bear up the best she could and not wish away these days. The worst thing that could happen is that they would be over too soon. An early baby was a guessing game and could bring sorrow.

This particular Saturday morning, at the beginning of February, she was sitting up. Ramsey had carried up the rocking chair and gingerly moved her to its cushioned seat. He cautioned her not to rock too much. Delphi hid her smile. He was more nervous than she was. The baby was huge, and she still felt its movement, but something had changed. It was as if everything was suddenly too crowded and instead of kicks and punches, there were only nudges and thumps here and there. She asked her husband to send for the doctor after explaining her thoughts. She was not afraid; she just wanted some reassurance.

Ramsey sent Ramy to the Little Hawk farm. Delphi didn't need to be left alone and Ramsey hoped to wait with her and see if David or Ox could go for the doctor. David was happy to oblige as Ox was courting and had gone to spend the afternoon in town with Pat, his sweetheart.

When Doc arrived, Delphi had already moved back to bed, her back ached terribly and she could not get comfortable. She had turned 15 in January, plenty old enough to birth, but she was petite and just plumb worn out. He felt her abdomen and took her pulse. She had broken out in a fine sweat but neither Delphi nor the doctor felt any signs of true contractions. Her ankles were a little swollen and painful, and her back was tight but that was all. She was given a tiny bit of laudanum and some aspirin and Ramsey put pillows beneath her ankles. And they were to send for Doc immediately if the back pain worsened or turned into gripping pains as this could be contractions.

Before the instructions were even finished, Delphi faded out and dozed into a pleasant sleep.

The pains began around dawn. Delphi sat straight up in bed out of a deep sleep.

"Get Ma."

Ramsey was already pulling on his britches and sliding into his boots. He made her as comfortable as possible, and they prayed a short prayer together before he rode the mule hell bent to the Little Hawk farm. Delphi tried to sing to herself and stay calm. She knew it was too early, but the doctor had assured her that many babies survived being born a little early. Somehow each chorus she sang turned into a tearful prayer.

It seemed like an eternity, but Ramsey was back with Ma in a very short time. They had sent Pa for the doctor and the little boys were on their way back with him now. Delphi was sitting up in bed talking to Doc the best she could. The pains were almost constant and made it very hard to concentrate or understand anything going on around her.

The sun was almost halfway up now, and Ramsey had been sent to the barn. Ma was standing by with clean hot water and sheets. The doctor was huddled at the edge of the bed looking over the situation and Delphi did not even care. She had to push.

"Now, girl, when you feel the pain get strong, I need you to breathe out and push until I say."

Delphi did as she was told, and tears rolled down her cheeks. Ma held her hand now and told her that David had come early, and Ox was late. Time was up to God. That helped some.

"Again, Mrs. Youngblood. Delphi! Push!"

Suddenly there was an immense feeling of relief. Ma leaned over and kissed her as the doctor held up the tiny dark bundle.

"A girl, Delphi!" He said, then quickly lowered the child to his lap.

"Neosha." Just that single word he spoke...Ma's name. And she quickly grabbed a sheet and took the baby from his hands. Delphi struggled to sit up. Silence. Why was everyone so quiet? Why didn't the baby cry? It looked as though both Ma and the doctor were rubbing the baby. Hard.

She was propped up on her elbows, craning to see. Just as she was about to ask for her daughter, another pain ripped through her core. She cried out.

"That's just the afterbirth," Doc said, "it will all be over in a moment." And he moved back to the edge of the bed.

But suddenly there was another pain and the now familiar relentless urge to push. The doctor said Ma's name again. She laid the baby in the cradle and moved to Delphi's side. Her face was stained with tears. Delphi wanted to ask. To see. But another pain tore her in two.

"Neosha? Can you come here and give me a hand please?" the doctor sounded oddly calm and quiet.

"What?" Delphi cried. In sheer terror, she finally found her voice. It was at that moment that Ramsey clattered in the door. He was white as a ghost.

"I heard the shouts. What has happened?" Ramsey stood over the cradle and his face fell. "Esther. Esther Patience, for she needed some of that." He looked at Delphi.

Another pain ripped again. The urge to push was unbearable. Then suddenly, the relief again. Doc was smiling broadly as he held up a second bundle. It was like a dream. Two? Delphi fell back against the pillow and sighed as a dark curtain closed over her. As she drifted away, she heard her Ma's voice.

"A girl. Another girl." This time, there was a lusty cry.

Ramsey was of two minds. He had never been so shocked and devastatingly confused. Not even when his Annie was taken so young by the flu that had rocked the entire community a few years ago.

Here he was holding his daughter, a joy beyond reason. But just there, in the beautiful handmade cradle was their Esther, the longed for, hoped for, prayed about blessing. And she had never breathed. Neosha said that her eyes had been open, but they were closed now, and the little lungs had never drawn breath. The baby girl in his arms wailed mightily. She was tiny, true, but still little Esther was even smaller. That is why Delphi had seemed so big. It wasn't a single large baby, but two mite sized ones.

This little one, raven hair and midnight eyes, just like her mama, was strong. She kicked her feet and screamed at the world. She had suddenly been plunged from her warm nest and ripped from her sister all in one dazzling sweep.

Ramsey's eyes and attention shifted to the bed for a moment. Delphi's Ma and the doctor were whispering at the head of the bed, and casting concerned glances at Delphi. He saw Neosha lower her eyes and move her mouth…a silent prayer.

"Delphi?" Ramsey's voice came out shattered and rough.

"She will be alright. In a while, "Doc said, "she has just used all her strength and lost some blood. And then there will be the shock of the first child. It's not unusual when we have the surprise of twins. One is often smaller and weaker. Rarely does either survive when the pregnancy is undiagnosed. But I didn't see it. Delphi is just so petite. I never heard the second heartbeat, I just thought we were on track for one robust baby."

Doc had given her something to sleep, though she likely didn't need it after her effort. And he was leaving more laudanum at the house for the first few days of rest and grief, should it be needed. In the meantime, Ma would stay and help with the new baby. Though strong, the infant was tiny and would need constant attention. They would need to milk the cow and feed the baby from a dipped rag until Delphi was stronger and the baby could suck. For such a small girl, the baby's color was good, and she was moving a lot. The doctor seemed sure of her survival. As sure as he could be, so early on.

The other precious package was wrapped in the beautifully delicate pink blanket and lying in the oak cradle. Not today, but tomorrow, the family would gather and place her in the burying ground in a tiny box. The hurt was cold and deep but balanced with the shocking gift of a second life. It was hard to reconcile such feelings. Everything was confusing and tiresome. If it was so hard on the family and Ramsey, how would Delphi manage when she came back to herself? God, pray she DID come back to herself. The doctor would be stopping in tomorrow and every day thereafter until mother and baby were in a rhythm nursing and sleeping with little pain.

And the baby, the second girl, would need her mother more than most. Her size and her loss, the early birth…this baby would need plenty of love. And a name.

Delphi did not have much energy to talk to the family. She held her tiny daughter close and whispered to her whenever she was awake. And she had words of love and encouragement for her sons. But for some reason, she just did not have conversation for Ma or Ramsey or anyone else, for that matter. Some of it was deep thought. She had just been through more than she could ever imagine. All the grief and hurt of what had happened all those months ago on that summer day…all the betrayal and hurt over her older sister…gone. Completely out of her mind. This newest pain was black and angry and disappointed. And she felt that she had let her husband down in some way. And that she had failed her Esther.

But this. This tiny brown creature was her whole world. She breathed still because of it. She still sang because of this baby. She still prayed and ate and slept for this child. And this girl needed a name. Days turned into a week, and finally she felt almost resolved.

Ramy was reading in the corner and Little Joe sat on the foot of the bed and played with his sister's toes.

"Joe Joe, go get your pa, please."

The young boy hopped off the bed and scampered out of the room. Ramy looked up. Ma's voice was louder and stronger. He had quietly watched her with fear for several days now. She was only content if he, his brother, and the new baby were all in the room. He rushed through his chores, so he could sit with her. And he spent his time thinking of conversation and tales to tell her. His other Ma had been gone and that was a hole in his heart. He needed Little Mama, and he wanted to do all he could to make her better.

Ramsey now stood in the doorway and watched as Joe climbed back up on the foot of the bed.

"Careful son don't jostle Little Mama," he gently cautioned his youngest boy.

He looked on his little family with love and concern. Things were not right yet. But he was hopeful that she had sent for him. The look on her face was not quite a smile, but it was an improvement. Even in all her grief and confusion she had refused to take the sleeping medicine and she was attentive to all three children.

"Sweetheart, what can I do?" He moved to the rocking chair. Delphi turned to face him and took a deep breath. She let it out in one long whistle.

"I reckon she needs a name, and I have pondered it for days. Ophelia. Ophelia Winsome. Because she IS a pretty little thing, and a blessing. Like the sun after a storm." Delphi fell quiet again.

Ramsey rubbed his head and smiled. This was a good sign, he knew. Ophelia. He liked that.

"That'll do just fine," he said.

Spring turned to summer and summer to fall. Ophelia was a happy, healthy baby that loved being outside. She was so easy to manage and never cried. She watched her brothers with rapt attention, and they adored her as well. The little family could not have been happier.

Delphi was outside in the garden picking snap beans. She had planted the corn, beans, and pumpkin in a Three Sisters Garden, just as Ma had taught her. The corn was tall, and the pumpkin vines were creeping. The beans were plentiful and just what she needed to go with the hog they slaughtered. Bacon and beans were one of her boys' favorite meals. Today was Saturday, and she would make enough to have for after church tomorrow.

Taking the family to church filled her and Ramsey both with pride. The boys were well behaved and so sharp. And little Ophelia was bright eyed and attentive. Many people commented on their children and Delphi took this as high regard. There was nothing more important to her than to be a fine wife and have intelligent, hardworking, God-fearing children. Ramsey was very content with her and treated her with respect and kindness.

Others in town and out near the farm might guess about their strange beginning, but it would be hard for anyone outside the family to know the whole truth. And the way things had turned out made it easy to brush the past under the rug. People didn't ask about Jetty. That was family business. And after a year, few thought about Mr. Joseph, the traveling preacher that had only been with them a few months.

Delphi was firmly and securely Mrs. Youngblood with the home and family to mark it.

Days passed pleasantly and with purpose. Her butter and egg business was thriving. Not only did she have her transactions with the store in town, but some of the neighbors had taken to buying her butter. It was good quality, and she had an abundance. Ramsey's farm was successful too. He worked from sun up to sundown and came in hungry, tired, and happy.

After Delphi was done in the garden, she gathered up Ophelia and Little Joe and walked to the Little Hawk farm. Ramy and Ramsey would be in the fields for a time, yet, and she had a moment or two to visit with Ma.

As she came into the kitchen in the front part of the house, she saw Ma sitting at the table. Her head was in one hand and the other held a letter. She could see Ma was distressed.

"Ma...are you well? Do I need to get someone?"

Ma looked up with strain showing on her face and held the letter out to Delphi...

Ponca City, Oklahoma

September 24th, 1899

Dear Ma and Pa,

We are getting on well. After staying some time with Joseph's father and brother we have come to the Osage Reservation in Oklahoma. There are Quapaw people here too. Most everyone is friendly, and many keep the old ways best they can in this day. You would be happy here, Ma.

Joseph has arranged for a little house, and we hope to be settled here for some time. You can be happy for me. I am going to be a mother. The little one should come any day. I do miss you sometimes, but Joseph says my place is here and that God is leading us. He tries to find a new church, but it is not so easy. Pray for me and my baby. I will write more when our child comes.

Your daughter,

Jettimae

Delphi handed the letter back to her mother. She was filled with sadness and confusion.

"They likely came very close thru here to pass to the reservation," Ma said quietly.

"Yes," said Delphi, "and she says nothing about marriage. That is a thorn."

Ma and Delphi discussed the letter at some length and resolved to pray for Jetty. It was a hard thing to swallow, the thought that she could travel so close without a meeting. The thought that Joseph was still controlling her life. And the fact that she was technically unmarried, pregnant, and a stranger far away in a distant town. They felt for her but were helpless to do anything.

Delphi went home that night and made supper for her boys. Then they all set on the porch and talked of the day. Tucking the boys in bed that night, swaddling Ophelia, and praying with Ramsey, Delphi knew that her choices were sound, and her heart was right. But she ached for her sister.

3

Years pass swiftly when children are young. There is a rhythm to the sweetness of the days. Every milestone is bright and new and marked with celebration.

Ramsey was in high cotton. Ramy was all but a man at 14 and did a full man's day of work. They had cleared out 10 more acres and the harvests were proof of their efforts. Ramy was all talk of building his own home of the back part of the farm and striking out a bit. Little Joe was not so little anymore and was bound for a life with the church. That was Delphi's influence. She had taught the boy a strong steady faith and always lifted the family up in prayer.

Beautiful Ophelia. She was her own creature. Much like her ma. At four she was fiercely independent and had a wild, brave heart. Yet she was a good little girl. Obedient and oh, so smart.

There had been some sorrow. A baby boy had come too soon, two winters ago. He had not opened his eyes. He now rested next to Esther awaiting a reunion in Heaven.

But Delphi nursed a brand-new son, Seth. He was strong and healthy. Quiet, like Ramy and showing signs of taking after Ramsey's tall height. These were the joys that filled Ramsey's mind as he rode his horse into town. A neighbor had stopped by this morning with a message: there was something waiting at the depot for the Little Hawk family. Delphi's pa was a bit under the weather, so Ramsey had offered to go.

Alpena Pass was bustling. The last few years had shown great growth for the town. Trains now stopped twice a day, and folks from all over used the stations for goods, travel, and mail. Buildings were going up and roads were going down. It was not just a wide spot in the line anymore. Theis meant great things for the farmers in the area. Grain, produce, and livestock turned a profit never seen before, as they could be sent to market far and wide. Yes, Ramsey was in high cotton.

Clouds were gathering above as Ramsey trotted his mule up main street. He nudged her towards the depot as he looked around. There were now two hotels and many new stores lining the little downtown street. With the expansion of the train schedule, there were strangers in town. Some were travelers, some were conducting business. Except for these visitors, Ramsey knew everyone he met and greeted them all in a friendly manner.

The depot was busy. It was just a bit after noon and Ramsey was anxious to make this pick up and get back home to work.

He had chores to finish and then he needed to head over to the Little Hawk farm to help Delphi's sick father. The two families shared work and enjoyed greater benefit of the communal yield. Ramsey felt very fortunate to have married into such a lively, honest, giving family. He felt that there was nothing he would not do for his wife, children, and in-laws. So, he was happy to run this errand and help out any way he could.

Once he entered the depot, he looked around. He did not readily see anything that he could identify as some kind of delivery for his father-in-law. So, he made his way up to the station master's office to make inquiry. He knocked at the little half door and waited. As he stood there, he heard voices inside. It sounded like a small child was babbling his numbers.

Mr. Grady stepped to the door and opened it.

"Come inside Mr. Youngblood. I expect you're here for Atsadi Little Hawk?"

"Afternoon, Grady. Yes sir. Seems something important came for them on the train?"

"I'd say so, Mr. Youngblood. And it wasn't likely to wait."

Mr. Grady moved aside. Behind him, a small dark boy sat on a salt barrel. He was roughly Ophelia's age. Maybe a wee bit younger. He was dirty. Grimy, even. Barefoot and barely dressed in a meal sack tunic. There was a paper pinned to the hem of his makeshift garment. And he was Native. Ramsey swallowed hard. He couldn't help but stare. The little fellow looked JUST LIKE OPHELIA.

The little mite looked up at Ramsey silently. Mr. Grady stepped forward and unpinned the paper from his clothing. He just shook his head as he handed it to Ramsey.

> Please deliver my boy to the Little Hawk farm at Denver, Arkansas. His name is Thomas Tall Chief, and he is 3 years old. He eats good and does not get sick. His pa has left, and I cannot feed him anymore. He is a good boy and knows his prayers. His Granny will know who he is.

And that was all.

Ramsey looked at his feet and shook his head. This was beyond peculiar.

"I don't reckon you got a look at anybody he might have been with?"

Mr. Grady frowned and shook his head.

"No sir, but I asked around and there was an Indian woman, what took a meal at the old hotel this morning. She left out on the return train to Oklahoma. I reckon it was…"

Ramsey covered his face with his hand and sighed.

"…Jetty."

Ramsey squatted down before the little Osage boy.

"Thomas, I sure am sorry, boy. But it gets better now."

Ramsey looked up at Mr. Grady with a stern, solemn glance.

"Don't be talking, Grady. It ain't fair to the boy. Besides, everyone will put it together soon enough. And I thank you."

With that, he lifted the little boy up and carried him out of the depot. A fine drizzle had started, and Ramsey thought glumly about the ride home and how miserable the entire situation was. Thomas lifted a grubby little hand up to Ramsey's cheek. The little boy pulled a frown. Ramsey realized that he was copying the tall man's own face. Quickly, they both smiled.

Along the ride home, it was obvious that Thomas had sat a mule or horse many times before. The little boy was silent no matter how much Ramsey tried to get a response from him. But little Tom did not seem sad, or worried in the least. This was even more troubling. What child of three or so could brave such a journey and separation so well? It didn't say much for whatever life he had left. How sad.

Ramsey said a quiet prayer for guidance, strength, and courage. Thomas looked at him very seriously and then spoke for the first time since he had counted his numbers at the depot,

"Amen."

Ramsey smiled.

Ramsey decided in the moment and guided his mule towards home. The little boy would need a wash and something to eat. He was sure to fit into something of Ophelia's or cast offs from Joe. Either way, he needed a change of clothes as well. And shoes. Ramsey shook his head, wishing he had thought to stop in the store in town. But truth be told, he was a bit muddle headed and shocked about the whole ordeal. And there was no doubt that Neosha and Atsadi would feel the same way. This would pierce their hearts.

Over the years, they had all wondered and sorrowed when they did not hear from Jetty again. Delphi and her mother had expressed the hope that they would see her and her child someday. They had worried and mourned over her future with a villain like Mr. Joseph. But none of them had dreamed that Jetty would come so close without direct contact. And to leave her young son.

Delphi would know what to do.

And she did. As they dismounted in the front yard, Delphi had blinked, eyes wide and questioning. She squatted down to the little one's height and then read the note that Ramsey held out to her. She read quickly, and just shook her head.

"Well, there Thomas, are you hungry?"

Thomas nodded his head and followed Delphi into the house. As he tucked into biscuits and jam, Ramsey and his wife quietly discussed the matter. It was quickly decided that they would journey over to the Little Hawk farm after chores. And they both agreed that Thomas might belong more readily in their home than that of his grandparents. They were finally alone, with all their children grown. Pat and Ox had married 3 years ago and had two small sons at home, soon expecting another mouth to feed. David had moved down the road and built himself a nice little cabin. He was courting Miriam Thomas, the middle daughter of their preacher. Delphi and Ramsey were in accord.

They would offer to give Jetty's little boy a home. But this was something the entire family needed to decide.

Ramsey went back to the fields and he and Ramy worked quickly, in a rush to finish all the chores so they could head to the Little Hawk Farm. Delphi sent Joe on the mule to ask both David and Ox to join them at their parents' home that afternoon. Then she started her efforts to make little Tom comfortable and clean.

She brought Ophelia and Tom into the yard behind the house. As she sat on the ground with Seth, Ophelia wandered around the grass. She joyfully pointed, naming off the chickens, dog, and horses for her smiling cousin.

Then Delphi offered them cookies and sat silently near, listening as Tom and Ophelia began to exchange information. Ophelia was a thoughtful little girl and spoke quietly and slowly, like her mother.

"I'm Filia. I have brothers."

"Yep," Tom replied.

"My Daddy has this farm. Mommy has eggs."

"My pa is gone," Tom said. "Ma is done. This is hard, and she isn't doing it."

Ophelia placed her dark arm around her cousin and offered him her cookie, "Yes."

They were quiet for a moment. Then Ophelia leaned in close and whispered.

"You can stay with me. What's your name?"

"Tom...okay."

Delphi felt a burning sadness. What had Jetty suffered to bring her to this? What woman would cast off her own child?

Delphi had done her best to clean up little Thomas. A pair of Joe's old britches were cut off to fit, and a shirt, though a bit big, managed to complete his outfit. It was still quite an improvement on the grain sack he had come in.

The Youngblood family loaded up in the wagon and headed over to the Little Hawk farm. The smaller children giggled at startled birds and made-up imaginings. Ramy and Joe watched in curiosity.

As they pulled up into the front yard, Atsadi and Neosha came out on the front porch. David and Ox were already there. Pat had stayed home, big in her last month of pregnancy. All eyes were focused on the group dismounting from the wagon. Atsadi came down the steps to help tie off the mules.

"Ramsey, I thank you for your trouble. There was something at the depot in Alpena?"

Ramsey turned just as Delphi lifted Tom down from the wagon box. He held tightly to her with one hand and clung to Ophelia with another.

Delphi looked her Pa in the eye, "Pa, this is Thomas Tall Chief. His mother brought him on the train. She departed before Ramsey arrived at the depot. But she left this letter."

With that, Delphi handed the tragic note to her father. Atsadi read it quickly, then passed it to Neosha who had come to stand with them in the yard. She too read the note and her face froze in a pained frown. She bent down and lifted the little boy up and carried him to the porch. Sitting down in her rocker, she began to whisper in his ear.

The men broke off to help Atsadi with the chores and the women and children joined Neosha. By the time the men returned, Delphi and her mother had discussed the situation and arrived at the only logical conclusion. Thomas would join the Youngblood family and take their name. Tall Chief was no legacy to maintain. Ma and Pa Little Hawk would gladly join in his raising as doting grandparents. And Jetty would be prayed for, worried about, and pitied. Why she had not come with Tom to stay, they would never know. David and Ox were especially critical of their missing sister. But Delphi still wondered how much of the truth they did not know.

They all gathered in the kitchen for a quick supper of biscuits and sausage gravy. Then the Youngbloods loaded up into the wagon and headed home in the twilight. The two toddlers fell asleep on the way, exhausted from their exciting day.

Once home and everyone to bed, Delphi and Ramsey lay in the dark, recounting the events of the day. No one could have imagined this outcome, but neither of them was truly surprised. They were just grateful that Thomas had arrived with no great harm.

Very few questions were asked at church and in town. It was not unusual for the children of relations to be raised by family. Poverty, illness, and death made needs must. Thomas was simply introduced as "our boy Tom Youngblood." His unfortunate beginning and parentage would not follow him into his life. He'd had enough challenges so far. Tom grew quickly with good food in his belly and love in his heart. He clung to Ophelia, and she to him. It was almost as if the space in her soul, left by her lost twin was made whole when she gave her care to her cousin.

Tom took after Delphi and Ophelia somewhat. He was a quiet watchful child. He listened more than he spoke. His voice was seldom heard unless it was raised in song, prayer, or small secrets with Ophelia. The adults wondered at his resilience. The child did not seem to have nightmares. He never cried or showed any fear. He never asked questions and he had not once mentioned his mother or asked about his father. He was a contented little boy. It would serve him well.

The sun was low in the afternoon sky when a stranger came into view on the dirt road. Ramsey and the older boys were just coming in from the fields. Ox had traded work and spent the day on the Youngblood farm helping out. Pat and Delphi sat on the porch shelling beans while Seth and Pat's small daughter played on a quilt in the front yard. Tom, Ophelia, and their two cousins were out back chasing chickens.

The dogs began to bark as the stranger turned down the lane toward the farmhouse. Delphi stood and shaded her eyes with her hand, trying to make out just who the man was. She turned and went in the house as Pat called for the men.

Ramsey led the boys from the barn and stood to welcome their visitor. His smile disappeared when he realized just who was come to see them. Joseph Tall Chief rode high on a bay stud. His clothes were filthy, and his face was iron.

"I reckon you've got something of mine."

Ramsey's voice was cold and even.

"No. No sir. Me and mine."

Joseph came off his horse and stepped toward Ramsey. Ox took a step forward and stood shoulder to shoulder with Ramsey and Ramy. Little Joe picked up Seth and the baby girl and headed around the house.

Joseph Tall Chief planted his feet wide.

"That no good woman may have shuffled him here, but he's mine and I'll have him, thank you. It's no use making things hard. Law's on my side."

Ramsey clenched his fists and squared his jaw. But just as he was ready to make a move, he saw Joseph's eyes go wide. Then the awful man took a step backwards. His startled gaze was fixed beyond Ramsey's shoulder.

Everyone turned.

There stood Delphi, all 5-foot naught of her, training her husband's 30/30 Winchester on Joseph Tall Chief's cold heart. Her hand was steady as she slid one into the chamber. Her voice was steady too.

"Remove your hat when you are in the presence of Christian ladies."

The vile man quickly removed his hat. He was shaking, and he dropped it in the dirt. Pat let a nervous giggle escape. Joseph looked shamed, but he never took his eyes away from the barrel of the gun.

Delphi's next words were quiet and even.

"There is nothing here for you. Everything here belongs to my man. Now you just go on. We'll not see you here again."

Joseph took up the bay's reins, but he did not turn around. He backed up the lane until he was out of view.

Delphi stood stock still until he disappeared. Then Ramsey moved to her and lifted the gun out of her hands. She turned her eyes up into his. She had no words. But he placed a loving hand on her shoulder.

"I know, Little Mama. I know."

He bent down and kissed his wife and they all moved into the kitchen to pray and eat.

Thomas had not seen. He had not known. And more importantly, the evil man had not laid eyes on Thomas. Or Ophelia.

Life marches on. Some fractures heal, and some become part of the landscape. People are either broken or made stronger by their wounds.

Delphi took her hurt and created love. She grew her family and concentrated on her husband and children. She was so proud of her sons and daughter. As time passed, the Youngblood brood filled an entire pew in the Denver Community Church. Their voices swelled with hers and rounded out worship on Sunday mornings.

Ramy stood as tall as his father now. He lived in the cabin he had built on the edge of the farm back in the trees. He had a sweetheart named Maggie Burns. They had marriage plans for the spring. Delphi looked forward to having another young lady in the family. Maggie was a good girl. Her folks lived just outside of Alpena Pass and her father worked on the railroad. Ramsey had gone to school with her mother and the two families got on well.

At 16, Little Joe was no longer little. He was done with grammar school now. The other men in the family had worked hard to see that Joe made it all the way through to graduation. Joe himself had taken a job in town during the summers and they had all saved. He would be leaving next year to Virginia for college. No one from their community had ever gone or even been accepted to such a fancy university as William and Mary College. Delphi and Ramsey were in awe of Joe's intelligence and accomplishments. That boy would make a name for himself. His heart was still for the Lord, and he was intent on changing the world.

Ophelia was a quiet beauty. She saw everything around her and had such a big heart. She helped her mother with the other children and the home. She was a reader but enjoyed needlework and being outside more. She was a graceful flower, surrounded by doting brothers. But her little world revolved around her Tom. She seemed aware of his every thought and move. It was as though she had taken on a special duty of his spiritual caretaker.

Tom was entirely different than when he had come to live on the Youngblood farm. He quickly grew strong and overcame any issues caused by his questionable start in life. He helped Ramsey and Ramy in the fields and did his chores satisfactorily and promptly. But he was queerly silent, and never still. The minute he was released from his tasks, he would disappear for hours on end. And he offered no explanation and answered no questions. No one knew where he went or how he spent his time, except possibly Ophelia. And when he was out of sight, she was tense. As if she was only content when she could keep an eye on Tom. He wandered and Ophelia worried. What bothered Delphi the most was that Tom never seemed as concerned about her as she was about him. So, Delphi prayed for them both and turned it over to the Lord.

Delphi was a busy momma. Young Seth was now 4 and learning to read. He had Delphi's large black eyes and Ramsey's curly brown hair. He laughed and played and sang and filled the silences left by his older siblings. He pattered about with the animals and seemed to have a special touch with them. In addition, two more small sons rounded out the domestic happiness.

William and Samuel toddled about, hands in everything, requiring any extra attention Delphi might have spared.

Their days were long, and Delphi was often tired when she lay down in her husband's arms at night. Their love burned stronger as the years went on. They had built a home, a family, and a life together. After a time, neither even thought about the dark time that had brought them together. As Delphi had once noted, 'beauty from ashes."

It was a bright spring Saturday, and Ophelia was more than a little excited to be spending it away from home. This morning she had helped her mother feed the growing family and pack them off for their day. Then Ma had given her an extra biscuit and patted her on the head.

"Give Iko and Agiduda my love." And with a kiss to her Ma's cheek, the young girl was out the door.

Her father, Tom, and Ramy were headed off to the field to continue planting. Papa worked hard, and so did the boys. Every year they planted wheat, corn, and tobacco. There were peach trees too. And a very large vegetable patch. But she and her Ma did most of the work in the garden. And then there were the chickens, pigs, and cows. It took a lot of hard work to feed their family. But they all pitched in and often had much profit to show for the effort.

Now she had three little brothers and a new baby sister as well. Bonnie was such a round, happy, little girl. She had the same black eyes as other women in the family, but her hair was soft brown and wavy like Papa's. She hardly ever cried, and

Ophelia enjoyed caring for her and dressing her up. Seth, Will, and Sam were a busy, messy, loud crowd of boy-ness. They took up much of her spare time because Ma needed her help. She felt that she never got to read or sew enough. That didn't really matter, though. She loved them all and they adored her.

But today, she was skipping off to her granny Iko Neosha's house. Even big girls needed a day off. Iko and grandpa Agiduda Atsadi's back field was just on the other side of the orchard. Ophelia liked to climb the fence and walk past the creek on her way to see them. All the birds and little animals went ahead and scampered around as if she wasn't even there. She was careful not to startle them. This was THEIR home, and she was the visitor. Iko had taught her that. She practiced not leaving a track or trace and was getting better and better at making the trip in silence. She couldn't wait to tell Iko about the little rabbit she had just almost touched.

Ophelia threw her hand up in a signal to her Agiduda. He was following his draft horse up and down the rich dark furrows. She dug in her pinafore pocket for the carrot Ma had given her. The Belgian was a big, golden, lumbering baby. Sometimes Agiduda would lift her and her brothers up on to its long sway back. They could all fit, one behind the other. She stopped for a moment, gave her grandpa a smile, fed the horse, and ran the rest of the way to the house.

As she pushed her way in the front door, Ophelia called out,

"Iko Neosha?"

"Come in, Child."

There she was. Neosha stood tall and straight in the middle of the kitchen. She was weaving her long black hair into a braid. Her granny had the longest hair Ophelia had ever seen. It reached down past Iko's behind. And it was dark as night even though she was getting on in age and her face was lined.

When she was done, Neosha went on tiptoe and reached the top shelf. She brought down an earthen bowl. It was worn completely smooth and shiny with use. Then she brought down a box and handed it to her granddaughter. Neither one of them spoke as they walked from the kitchen into the back bedroom and out the door into the rear yard.

They both folded their legs and lowered themselves to the ground. Neosha placed the bowl between them and took the box from Ophelia. She took out a bundle of sage leaves and placed it in the bowl. Then she lit a match and held it to the sage until it truly caught and began to smolder. They both watched silently as the bowl began to smoke.

Iko closed her eyes and began to speak as she made signs with her hands,

"Long ago, the People were stars. They lived in the sky. Sun was their father and Moon was their mother. There was peace. But the People grew restless and wanted change. Mother Moon told them to fly down and seek a new home. The People rode on the back of a raven all the way down to Earth. But the Earth was covered with water. The only place for the raven to roost was in the tops of seven tall trees that grew out above the water.

This was an adventure, but the People still sought more. They looked all across the waters on the Earth and the wisest bravest animal they saw was Red Elk. They called to Red Elk, and he came to help. Red Elk lay down in the water and rolled about. The waters drew back from him and showed dry land. The People were blessed. Then they saw that everywhere Red Elk stepped, trees, crops, grasses and medicine plants grew. These were gifts from Red Elk to the People. And this is how the world began."

Ophelia watched her grandmother's face. Iko Neosha was so smart. She knew all the secrets about Everything. Her people had been here longer than anyone else's people. Ophelia knew that was special and that she herself was a part of that great history. It was important that she remembered all these things that her granny told her. That way, Ophelia's children would know the stories too.

Before Neosha had married grandfather, she had lived on a place called a reservation. This was land that the government gave to the Osage. But it wasn't a gift. It was land meant to hold the Native people in one place and away from the white settlers. There was oil under the Osage land that the government wanted. So, they had taken it from the People. Iko was sad when she talked about the reservation. Long before that, the Osage and other tribes had lived on ALL the land in America. It was one big homestead from ocean to ocean. The elders had been able to go wherever they wanted, following game and gathering medicine. Ophelia knew that her granny, her granny's ma, and all the women before them had special talents with medicine and special ties to everything around them, the Earth Spirits, and the Great

Creator. Now, the government men sent Iko and all the Osage people a lot of money every month. They thought they were paying the People for the oil. But Earth owned the oil, not the Osage.

Even though they could not live the way their elders had lived, at least they were still the same People, children of the Sky and Middle River. They were still blessed by Red Elk. No government could take that away for any amount of money.

Neosha sighed and opened her eyes. She looked long and hard at Ophelia.

"Remember."

Sundays were special. The whole Little Hawk family would meet at church and then gather at one of the farms for the afternoon.

Neosha and Atsadi liked to host. They were getting older and were comfortable at home. They enjoyed all their grandchildren and proudly watched the family grow. Ox and Pat had their two boys and daughter. David had married Miriam Thomas and they were expecting their second, with a small son already welcomed. And of course, Delphi and Ramsey filled the little house to the rafters with their large brood. Ramy and his bride Maggie rounded out the happy gatherings. The cousins ran about the yard willy nilly playing made up games and shrieking merrily. It was a time of joy for the adults as well. They helped watch each other's children and caught up on the crop progress, family news, and county gossip.

Inevitably, Jetty's name would come up now and again. They were a large clan, but there was a gaping hole left by the missing sister. With Tom now safely nestled in the family, it was Jetty's fate and safety that tore at them. Almost nine years had past since the boy's confounding arrival at the depot. And not one single word from his mother in all that time. Every letter sent to the council on the Reservation near Ponca either came back unopened or received no answer at all. The last contact of any kind had been the day Delphi ran Mr. Joseph off the property.

Atsadi began to talk of making a trip to the Oklahoma reservation. The older he got, the more his missing daughter weighed on his mind.

"Might be someone would remember her if asked face to face," he mused.

Ox let out a deep breath.

"Pa, I don't think you should go alone, maybe David and I could trip out there after the harvest."

Ramy and Ramsey immediately offered to watch the brothers' farms.

Atsadi thought this a good idea and admitted it would ease him to know they had tried all they could to find out her whereabouts. Tracing Joseph Tall Chief's family was out of the question. It could only lead to conflict and that was best left alone.

Ramsey called Delphi and Neosha away from the kitchen where the women were about ready to lay the lunch. Once consulted, Delphi agreed that it was a fine plan, but made sure no one would mention any of it to Tom. He had never asked about either of his parents. He didn't need to be burdened with the sad story when he was so well settled and loved. In the meantime, Delphi meant to write to the Native American registry offices in Oklahoma, Missouri, Kentucky and here in Arkansas. She was sure that Jetty would have made certain to stay current on an address valid for receipt of her oil benefits. Neosha willed a tired tense smile.

Delphi and her mother left the men on the porch and walked back in the house. Talk in there was still on Miriam's pregnancy and how much she wished for a girl. Boys were fine, but girls directly alleviated the burden on a woman and gave her company for a lifetime. The women worked like a well-tuned machine, buttering biscuits, slicing ham, and filling mugs. It was a small horde to feed, but it was old hat by now. Soon they would feed the men, then call in the children for their turn.

Monday would come, and school and the fields would call. Mending and washing, cooking and canning would be seen to. Each night there would be prayers and reading. They would all laugh and work and continue with their days. They measured their lives from week to week, birth to birth, and harvest to harvest. Each cog in the wheel turned busily so the operation ran smooth. But this day, at least for Neosha and Delphi, there was an empty shadowed corner where Jetty's presence loomed large.

It was November 1910. The leaves were coming down and it wasn't long until the holidays. The men had worked long and hard and put up a grand harvest. Delphi traded work with her sisters-in-law, Pat and Miriam, and Ramy's wife Maggie. They had canned the fruits and vegetables, put away butter and cheeses, and helped smoke meat. The whole family was ready for winter.

David and Ox had set out three weeks back for Kansas City, Missouri. After Delphi had written to the registry offices in all the surrounding states, an address had turned up for their sister, Jettimae.

It was an old hotel in Kansas City, specifically for maiden women and widows. Jetty was not exactly either of those, but her benefit checks had been going to that street address for the last three years. It had been a good lead. Good enough that it was worth the trip, and the men had set out with high hopes. Now they were back, alone. They had not found Jetty. But they had found the truth. And now, Delphi sat in her bedroom floor with a box. She would go over it all, put it away for Thomas, and try to carry on.

Delphi took a deep breath and pulled the top off the box. There was a handful of photographs on top. She thumbed through them and then wiped her eyes and looked more carefully. Here was a full-on photo of her sister. Jetty was not smiling but looked straight at the camera. It must be a few years old, but not many, because this version of her sister was different than Delphi remembered. Jetty had lines on her face, and she had lost weight. A lot of weight. She looked ill and hungry. There was a number scrawled across the corner of the picture. It must be a file picture of some sort. Some kind of identification snapshot. Then there was a picture of Jetty and Tom when he was newly born. He was wrapped in a tribal blanket and Jetty had hawk feathers in her hair. Maybe a celebration on the reservation. Perhaps Tom's naming ceremony. And then here was a picture of Jetty again, with a group of women. They were wearing hats and standing in front of a building. She was not smiling here either.

Deeper in the box was a stack of uncashed benefit checks, dating back to February 1908. They were tied with a piece of twine. Just on top of these was a beautiful strand of beads-red, black, and orange. It was a fine piece of work. Maybe done by Jetty herself? And here was Jetty's doll. The partner to the one Delphi kept in her rocking chair. Ma had made them both so very many Christmases ago. Delphi took it out and held it to her cheek. She thought she would have tears, but she only felt hollow inside. Dry. Like an empty husk.

She and Jetty had played house, made believe they were grown ladies with babies and husbands. They had sung songs together, joining their voices in harmony, like Ma had taught them. They shared the same bed and whispered under the covers at night. They worked together, learned to can, sew, weave, and cook. Delphi laid the doll aside and looked at her hands.

She was 25. Her hands were still strong, though calloused. The simple gold ring on her left hand reminded her that she was loved. She was a mother. To her children and also to her sister's boy. She put her face in her hands. Then she took another deep breath and turned back to the box.

There were two newspaper articles. The first was marked January 16th, 1908, and published out of the Kansas City Sun. Just a few lines under the crime report list.

```
—An unidentified Indian woman
was found deceased in the field
off West 2nd Street early Sunday
morning. The woman was wrapped
in a blanket and appeared to be
in her mid-20s. No crime is sus-
pected. Manner of death cited as
weather and liquor.
```

The second article was dated February 2nd of the same year, also the Kansas City Sun. It was a little longer. It said that Jettimae Little Hawk had been reported missing from her boarding establishment a few weeks earlier, and that it was suspected that she was the dead woman found frozen to death in a drunken stupor. It asked for any information or next of kin. The writer then went on to detail the alcohol and homeless problem with Native Americans in Kansas City. It named Jetty's death as the third such incident in 1908.

The last item in the box was a death certificate. It was dated and signed by the Kansas City Coroner. 'Indian Woman' was marked through, and Jettimae Little Hawk written above it. David and Ox had not found Jetty, but their testimony and information was enough to confirm for the sheriff that it was, indeed, Jetty, who had been found dead two years earlier. The doll among the belongings gathered at the hotel solved the mystery. They had not been able to find her grave, though. She had been put to rest in a common grave in the potter's field of the public cemetery.

Delphi sat for a few moments, waiting for the tears. They still did not come. She put the papers and the beads back in the box and pushed it under her bed. Then she stood up and stretched. The new baby was growing big and resting low in her belly. She was tired. And she still had supper left to get and tomorrow she would need to go see Ma. She bent over and picked up the doll. Then she crossed the room to her rocker and sat it next to its twin. What a sad and sorry thing.

4

The labor and birth had been difficult. Delphi whispered a prayer of thanks just to be through it. It was twins again, and this time, they both lay in the well-used cradle, sleeping peacefully. A boy and a girl. They were named for the grandparents: Ats and Nesa. Ramsey had agreed. They were tiny and brown and had been angry enough to squall themselves to sleep.

Delphi was exhausted and white as a ghost. She had hemorrhaged, and the doctor said there would be no more babies. Here in the country at a home birth, there was just no way to fix that. In fact, the survival of both babies and the mother was nothing short of a miracle. But with 10 living children and two in the grave, both Ramsey and his wife knew that was enough mouths to feed and they didn't grieve the lost future. They knew families with many more children than that. Some had one a year, and there was sickness, hunger, and death in those families. Delphi and her brood had been spared the worst.

Ophelia and Thomas were turning twelve. They were no longer children. Thomas and Seth were in the fields except for the short months of spring when they went to the grammar school. And Ophelia was not far off from a family of her own. In just a few years, some man would come courting and her life would start.

For now, Ophelia stayed busy helping Ma. William and Samuel were still in short pants and not quite ready for school. And Bonnie was in diapers. Now with the twins, Ophelia felt like a whirligig, running back and forth between the kitchen, the laundry, and helping Ma with feedings. Delphi had trouble with the twins. She had a hot hard spot that kept her from bringing her milk. Sometimes it made her so feverish and pained that she could not sit up in bed. Ramsey set Tom to milking the cow and Ophelia would boil the milk and take turns with the bottle for Ats and Nesa. It seemed one or the other was always hungry.

Delphi might be stuck in bed, but she was still Little Mama. She held court while Will and Sam practiced their numbers and letters. Bonnie loved to sit in the rocker and hold both the rag dolls there, just like Ophelia minded the twins. And then Seth would come in from school and quickly eat a biscuit and recount his day before joining the men in the furrowed fields. Tom went straight out to work.

Delphi made the best of her sick time by crocheting blankets and basting together shifts for the smaller children. She canted out an endless tutorial for Ophelia on the egg business and canning so that every Saturday, the girl could ride to Alpena Pass with her Papa and trade with the clerk at the mercantile.

Once Delphi felt better enough to be out of bed, she was still tired much of the time. She had lost a lot of weight and not gained an appetite. The doctor noted her difficult pregnancy and the trouble with the birth and said it would just take time to regain her strength and build her blood. He ordered liver and greens to give Delphi iron. That same day, Ramsey and Ramy butchered three hogs out of season just for the livers and headcheese. Little Mama was very important in the hearts of everyone she loved.

Neosha came daily to sit and rock and visit with Delphi and the children. She often brought her small brown bottle of turpentine. She would fetch a spoonful of sugar and then pour several drops of the evil smelling liquid on top. Then she watched, eagle eyed, as Delphi swallowed it down. Ophelia couldn't help but stamp her foot and gag. She knew just how that tasted. They all got dosed with turpentine in the spring to ward off worms. When you went barefoot on dew covered dirt, worms were a ready and present fear. It must work, for all the children were round and poly. But Little Mama never did seem to gain any weight.

Ophelia helped the best she could, cause Ma's chest and shoulder never did gain strength back or quit hurting. But it was good practice for her own home, Ma said. And Ma was always just there, over her shoulder, telling stories of the People, Red Elk, and Granny and Grampy's trip to homestead in Arkansas. And she filled Ophelia's head with Bible wisdom, and recipes, and remedies for every ailment under the sun. And Ophelia also learned a lot that Delphi didn't say out loud. About faith, and how to smile through pain to calm the children, and never complain. Sometimes Ophelia thought her Ma must be the kindest smartest woman in the world. She watched Ma soothe Pa and make him smile after a hard hot day. And Ma could hush the little ones with just a quiet word or even a silent look. And she knew every word to every hymn. She never missed church or forgot anything anyone told her. Ophelia thought that no matter how hard she tried, she would never be as perfect as Little Mama.

There were times when Ophelia felt that she fell short. Or that she made mistakes on simple tasks. It frustrated her to no end when she broke an egg or had to pick out her mending. It was these times when Little Mama said the wisest words of all. And they went straight to Ophelia's heart and nested there.

"Just be the best that you can be. God makes up for the rest." And Ophelia knew deep down that this had to be true. The words wrapped around her like a giant hug.

Tom was big for his age. And he was proud of it. He didn't have any hair on his face, like Pa or Ramy. Even Joe had a mustache when he came back from college in the East. But Agiduda assured young Tom that this was his Native blood. Cherokee and Osage men grew braids, not beards. And Agiduda Atsadi would tug on Tom's black mop of hair with a smile.

He could work a full day and run as many rows as Ramy or Pa. Or Uncle Ox or Uncle David, for that matter. He earned his keep and ate like a grown man according to Little Mama.

He knew somewhere way back in his mind that at one time, early on, he had a different Ma. So, he must have had a different father too, though he didn't truly remember either of them. His earliest memory was riding in front of Pa on a mule in the rain. And being happy. He had always had a warm bed and a full belly. He listened to Little Mama sing and he could read the Bible, though he wasn't much interested in any other reading or school. He knew numbers well enough to lay out a field and count a harvest, but beyond that, he got most his learning from the world around him. Everything was a cycle. Seasons and harvests. Births and deaths. You could tell what was coming from the color of the sky and the pelt on a deer. Tom loved his brothers and sisters. Especially Ophelia, though she asked too many questions and looked at him too hard. He felt like she could see his bones inside his skin, and when they just sat quiet together, she knew what he was thinking. So mostly, he liked to be alone.

After the work was done, he could take off to the creek and stand in the eddies and hand fish. Or quietly crawl through the tall grass and find bird eggs. When he brought these home to Little Mama, she always patted him on the back and thanked him for his provision. He didn't have many words, but he liked to bring her things, so she knew he loved her too.

Mostly though, Tom had taken to watching people. If he took off his boots and ran fast, he could make it to the rail yards outside town and spend most of Saturday watching folks. He was near sixteen now and wasn't above noticing a pretty girl out in front of the stores with her mother.

Tom had quit school at 14. It wasn't uncommon unless you were like Joe and headed to college or wanting to be a preacher or a doctor. Most of the big boys were needed on their family farms and learned what they needed to about providing and surviving. There were plenty of people around. Uncles, cousins, and the like. But he only saw ladies at church and town. Unless you counted Ma and the aunts. And Tom didn't.

He'd like to get married, but he didn't want a piece of the Little Hawk community. Nor Denver either. He wanted to find himself a golden-haired lady and take off on the railroad as far away as he could go. Maybe California. There was good work out there and lots of money to be made. All the family seemed happy as larks just to nest all next to each other and see the same faces and places year in and year out. But Tom knew there was a wide world out there. Farther even than Oklahoma. And a man could make his own name somewhere like that.

He felt a little pang in his heart when he thought of Ophelia. She always said they were tied, like the twins, Ats and Nesa. Two halves of a whole. But Tom didn't feel it. He didn't feel tied down to anyone or anywhere. He felt like a leaf on the wind, just itching to blow away. And that made him feel just an incy bit bad. He knew the story. Ophelia had lost her sister Esther right out of the womb. He reckoned that was why she clung to him so tight. It might hurt her powerfully when he left one day. But surely, soon, she would marry and have babies and she would be alright. It might feel like his lookout at times. But it wasn't. It wasn't. He reminded himself of that firmly.

On these off days when Tom could get to town, he always made his first stop at Big Red's shanty on the backside of Carrollton Street. Down by Long Creek, where it ran almost dry for the better part of the year, Big Red Harris had built his clapboard shack. There wasn't much to it, just a bed and a stove and a three-legged chair. But in the lean-to, now, there was something. There were jugs and copper tubes, and glass jars, and Tom still couldn't cipher what all. But it was complex and wonderful. You could see that for all Red's simple ways, his mind and his money were all tied up in that contraption in the lean-to.

Big Red sold shine. And Tom favored the Apple Jack kind. It was easy enough to get. Red liked the quiet Osage boy. He said hardly a word and just sat on the porch til it felt right. Then he'd lay a silver piece on the porch rail and Red would lead him to the still room. Just a little quart jar. And then off the boy would go until two weeks or so passed and he'd be back. And it would be just the same. Red never knew what Tom Little Hawk got up to, but he never heard of any trouble, so the boy must hold his liquor.

On this particular Saturday, Pa had left Tom to do as he pleased right after milking and feeding the pigs. They had spent weeks sowing the fields and then weeding and turning in the manure. Now it was what Little Mama called 'wait and see' time. And Tom was just pining for a day away, and unwatched.

He took his silver to Big Red and wrapped his jar in his handkerchief. Then he found a barrel on the front side of the depot and roosted on top, watching trains. His big brother Joe had got him in the habit of counting cars, and it was a mindless, soothing way to sip at his jar. Not that Joe would touch shine.

Best Tom knew, only Uncle David ever drank anything and that was to do what he called 'wetting the baby's head' anytime a new cousin was born. Beyond that, there was no drink anywhere on the Little Hawk homesteads. But Tom knew that as long as he didn't come home stinking of it, or get to fighting, then no one would be the wiser. Besides. It gave him some courage. And there was someone he was wanting to talk to.

For the third Saturday in a row, the pretty fair-headed girl was walking down the street with what had to be her mother. She wore a pink dress and gray kid boots. Her gold hair was tied up in a mess of curls that hung down between her shoulders. She looked straight ahead, not at her feet like so many women did. And sometimes her ma said something to her that made the girl throw her shoulders back and stand straighter. This girl was a person who might look you right in the eye. And she had come from some other place, he was sure. Because once, when he was brave with shine, he had crossed over the road and walked behind until they turned into the store. And he had heard them talk. It was a queer sound that came through their noses and none of the words were any he had ever heard. But then the mother greeted another woman on the sidewalk, and it was in perfect English. Yes, they were talking a foreign language between themselves.

Today, Tom was brave again, and he was going to say something to this beautiful girl. He was going to know her name. He was sure.

The Mercantile was packed. Women were fingering lengths of ribbon for new hats and men were trading tales and buying tobacco. Some of that tobacco was Tom's Pa's. He knew for sure.

He straightened his collar as he passed through the door. He had prepared. He was carrying a list sent by his Ma and the coin to make the purchase. He had sipped at his jar, but just enough to loosen his jaws and square his mind.

As he made his way to the clerk's counter, he made sure to pass close to the girl's ma. Close enough so he could look her in the eye and say,

"Scuse me ma'am. After you. Right nice day we are having."

The lady looked him over and gave a tight smile.

"Thank you, sir." She breathed out the words in her clipped nasally voice. But she had smiled.

Tom nodded at her daughter as well and was rewarded with a genuine smile that cut the girl's face from ear to ear. Her blonde curls framed wide light blue eyes and her smile showed in them as well.

As the mother read her list out to the clerk, Tom kept a few feet's distance but addressed the girl warmly.

"Tom Little Hawk. Welcome to town. I expect ya'll are new hereabouts?"

The girl inclined her head but kept her eyes on Tom's.

"Onni Jean Gerritsen. Yes. Just come from Tuscarawas, Ohio. But Mere and Pere are from France." Her voice came through her nose as well, but her words were slower and rounder. A little more like Tom's own English.

Tom let out a whistle. "France. My. That's far."

"Yes," Onni laughed, "But everyone is come to America now. And I was born in Ohio."

Tom made small conversation and then swallowed hard and invited the Gerritsen family to church. Onni made a small, puckered frown and told him that they were Lutheran and worshipped with other families in one another's houses. But then she said the words that made his heart sing.

"But we walk to town each Saturday. For the air. Every Saturday."

And with that, her mother turned, took up Onni's elbow and drifted out the door.

Tom stepped to the counter but could only pass Ma's list to the clerk. His mind was working much too fast for words.

5

Ramsey stood in the rear yard and looked out over the farm. He pulled off his hat, wiped his sweaty brow, and coughed. The grain was up. The peaches were ripe and needed picking. And the old boar truly should have already been butchered. There was that still to do and he might be tough. They'd have to brine some of the pork.

It would all have to wait. This afternoon, he would ride into Alpena Pass and collect Joe from the evening train. His education was complete, and he would come home for a nice visit before traveling West to start his church. Ramsey looked forward to seeing his son and was so very proud. But Little Mama was beside herself with excitement. She had been cooking and cleaning for days. Joe Joe was her special son, called by the Lord. She was walking on air.

Ramy had gone home to Maggie for the mid-day meal, and then he would finish the chores at his own home and here at the

Youngblood farm so Ramsey could make the trip. But Thomas was nowhere to be found and his help could really be handy. It wasn't like Tom to shirk his chores, but then again, it was happening more and more lately. Not even Ophelia had been able to tell her Pa where Tom had gone. She just pulled a confused frown and shrugged her shoulders. The girl was getting older and spent less time with Tom and more time helping Little Mama. It was a good thing too. Ramsey was worried about Delphi. She slept fitfully and moaned in her sleep. He knew that the knot in her chest hurt her, even though she never complained. It had worked its way into an open sore and the doctor kept her in salve and bandages. But she wouldn't take the opium or laudanum he left for her. She said it made her dizzy and she had no time for lying down. Ramsey thought it a hidden blessing that there were no more children, as Delphi had grieved over not being able to feed the twins. And another pregnancy might shrink her right down to nothing. She was already light enough to blow away.

He put his hat back on his head and went in the house. The little ones were all over him. Bonnie clung to his leg as the three middle boys talked a mile a minute, begging to ride to the depot with him. Nesa and Ats sat in Little Mama's lap in the rocker while Ophelia laid out the lunch.

"Any needs from town, Little Mama?" Ramsey asked as he rolled up his sleeves and tucked into the ham and potatoes his daughter set before him.

Delphi smiled her twinkling smile. She always had joy for Ramsey. It didn't matter if it was late, or if she was tired, or pained. Ramsey was grateful. She was the kind of wife that made a man respect himself and God's divine plan. She answered him in her even, quiet voice,

"Willow bark, husband. If there's no trouble. And calamine. There're eggs to go to the store, and I can send Ophelia if that's asking too much."

Ramsey thanked her for the thought and smiled at his daughter as well. Ophelia best stay here and help keep his little ones in line. It would not do to have Joe come home to a worn-out Ma.

The day was clear, and Ramsey made the trip in the wagon in good time. He beat the train by over half an hour and was standing expectantly when Joe stepped off. He was almost as tall as Ramsey. Dressed in a dark tailored suit and wearing a hat, he looked quite the part of a preacher man. He carried his carpet bag in one hand and his Bible in the other. Pretty as a picture, Ramsey wished Little Mama had felt well enough to ride in with him, if just to see the sight of her boy home from schooling.

Joe was full of news from the East. He was passing through headed to a small town in New Mexico where many Mexicans and Natives still practiced traditional spiritualism or Catholicism. He would join a group of Pentecost Missionaries already building a church and teaching farming and mathematics. His work and mission were very different than that of his stepmother's People. But he believed in it. And it was no secret that Little Mama was proud of him.

They had crowded the younger boys into one bed to make room for Joe while he was home. He spent time in the fields with his Pa, Ramy, and Tom. He told tales and played games with Will, Sam, and Seth. He set out one day and spent the whole of a morning with Iko and Agiduda Little Hawk. Then Sunday came, and Delphi walked proudly into church on her boy's arm. One last family Sunday dinner, and Monday morning, Joe caught the train out West. He would write, but they might not see him again for years and years. He was doing God's work, and Delphi trusted him to God.

She thought about teaching him his letters and the hymns so long ago. And those days when he was small enough to sit up front in the wagon on her lap and watch the trains when the family took their trips into Alpena. She closed her eyes and saw his little white hands folded in prayer and thought about his little bare feet. The pockets full of rocks and bugs, any small treasure he could give her. And she remembered the stories he made up for her when she was in bed waiting for Esther and Ophelia to be born.

He might have been brought into this world by another woman, but Joe Joe would always be her little boy. He taught her how to be a mama. God had given him to her when she needed him most, and now Delphi gladly gave him back to God.

Ophelia sat quietly in the pew. Bonnie sat beside her, twisting at her hem and Nesa was on her lap. It was so hard to keep her dress nice with little ones surrounding her. But she managed. And she knew that her gray frock with the thin red striping was very pretty. She had drawn it out on a newspaper, and Ma had helped her cut it out, but she had stitched it together herself. Her thick ebony hair was braided and pinned up in a cunning knot. She wasn't overly proud, she hoped. But she did feel pretty.

Pretty is as pretty does, said Granny Neosha. So, Ophelia composed her face into an attentive smile and tried to listen to the sermon, all the while bouncing the drowsy toddler Nesa on her knee and trying to keep Bonnie still.

There was a picnic today after services. Right there at the churchyard. It was Homecoming for the Denver fellowship. That meant that everyone, young and old had baked or cooked something and they would all eat together and visit until evening singing service. It was a big day and many folks that they didn't see regular would be there. It was also a chance for sparking.

Ophelia knew she was old enough. And she was plumb ready too. She loved her Ma, her Pa, and her little brothers and sisters, but lately she wanted her own house. Her own kitchen. And for someone to want to take her out walking. She wasn't all that much younger than her sister-in-law Maggie. And Maggie already had two babies. She had seen her brother Ramy kiss Maggie once, besides just at their wedding. He had come up behind her on the porch and wrapped his arms around her pregnant belly and kissed her cheek. It had made Ophelia blush. She didn't think she was supposed to see, and she didn't know where to look. But she knew then that she wished someone would kiss her someday too.

Preacher had finally ended his long benediction, and everyone was moving out the door. The little children were practically toppling over one another with their silly games and shrieking wildly. The men hovered under the big oak by the burying ground. But the women and older girls were laying out blankets on the ground and setting out plates and forks and food on the sawhorse and plank tables that were arranged near the building.

Ophelia joined a group of young ladies at the pie tables and set to slicing pieces of dessert. There were apple, peach, cobblers, and a chocolate cake that Ophelia had made herself yesterday. She beamed proudly when one of the granny's complimented its evenness.

Shortly, the men began to file through. Some of the girls chatted cheerfully between themselves. Ophelia smiled but didn't add much. She was a solemn girl and listened, like her mother. She knew these girls from the grammar school, and they got on well. But Ophelia had never been a talker.

She grinned at Papa when he came through and asked for a piece of her cake. She nodded to her uncles and her brother Ramy. There were other men in the church that she knew, and she dutifully handed out pie and sweets. She took a breath and wiped her hands on her apron. She rose up on tip toe and scanned the churchyard. Tom was nowhere to be seen. He had sat right in front of her during the service. But he was definitely not there now.

Just as the men were all through and the children started to come forward, she heard a low voice say her name.

"Ophelia," it was deep with a touch of a brogue, and it made her heart stop, "I'd kindly take a piece of your cake every-one's going on about."

As she placed a good-sized slice on the offered plate, she shyly looked up. The clearest pair of eyes she had ever seen were trained intently on her own black ones. These eyes weren't quite blue, nor gray even. They were truly clear. Like creek water, or an evening sky. They belonged to an angular face topped with riotous red curls. She had never seen this man before. And he was a man. Young, but older than her. His clothes were clean but worn. His hands were clean too, but large and calloused with square nails and used to working. She took all this in, but he never stopped looking at her face. Then he cracked a smile.

Ophelia went all liquid inside. Like butterflies and pussy-willows were tickling her gut and filling her throat. But somehow, this quiet girl, this still dark young lady managed to open her mouth,

"Gladly."

Thankfully, in an instant, her sister-in-law, Maggie was beside her. She put her arm around Ophelia and bubbled over,

"Filia, this is Dewey. Dewey Bailey. He's my cousin come from out East to work on the railroad. He's staying with me and Ramy til he puts away for a place. And he'll be coming to church."

Dewey smiled and took off his hat. Ophelia bobbed a little curtsy, and then bit her lip. She wasn't sure if that was right, but this beautiful boy with the ocean eyes was still smiling at her. Maggie took the knife from Ophelia's hand and tugged at the back knot of her apron.

"Here, trade me, Filia. Show Dewey over to the shade by the fence. He doesn't know anybody."

Blessed, babbling Maggie. She had that same red hair and a giant personality. Ramy said she had an Irish temper to match. But Ophelia had never seen Maggie be anything but happy and fun. Maggie quickly handed another fork to her cousin Dewey and said,

"Ya'll share that cake. It's big enough, and it'd be a shame if Filia didn't get to eat her own good works."

Ophelia bumped her shins on the sawhorse as she came out from around the table. Maggie's shove hadn't helped much. Dewey's hands were full of the plate, but he winged out an elbow and offered it to Ophelia. She felt like someone else as she slipped her hand in the crook of his arm and allowed him to lead her towards a tree.

They sat down and Ophelia's generally calm mind raced a mile a minute as she tried to conjure up something to say. But she needn't have worried. Dewey's musical brogue wove a tale about hopping a train car in Boston and all kinds of adventures that brought him there, that day, to her church.

Slowly, Ophelia began to smile, and giggle. She answered Dewey's polite questions and asked a few of her own. By the time they were called to go in for the singing, she knew about his trip from Ireland on the boat when he was only 5 years old. She knew about how he grew up outside of Boston raised by just his mother. How his father was killed in a factory accident. About how he had twelve...TWELVE brothers and four sisters.

And she had told him about Tom, and the little children, Granny and Grampy, catching rabbits, Red Elk, and even about Esther. Ophelia felt like she had never talked so much in her whole life. But she also didn't feel strange. It wasn't like Tom, where she had to measure words. Nor like Ma or Granny, where most of the talking wasn't done out loud, but down in their hearts. No, for the first time ever, she had traded words. Evenly. Like dealing out playing cards. And it was safe, and good.

It was Saturday, and Ramy and Maggie were coming across the field. Dewey was with them. He had his hat on, but those flaming curls were peeking out enough for Ophelia to tell it was him.

She patted her hair down and turned to Delphi,

"Ma, how do I look?"

"Pretty is as pretty does, 'Filia. But you look smart."

At that, Ophelia stepped onto the back porch and waved. The four of them were going on a picnic, and she just couldn't wait.

Dewey had been stopping in regularly, and Ma and Papa had been fine with it, as long as Maggie and Ramy came along. Ophelia supposed this was courting. Dewey hadn't said anything yet, but he was attentive, and they laughed together. Ophelia missed him during the week when he was on the railroad. But he always had such exciting things to share. Even though Ophelia didn't have much to talk about, Dewey made her feel like her world was interesting. He held onto every word that came out of her mouth.

And Sundays were best because they could sit and sing in church together. Then afterwards, even though they were walking with the whole family, they could hang back some and if felt like being all alone.

For the picnic, the four of them headed down to a grassy spot on the creek bank. Ma had helped Ophelia pack a basket with cold chicken, apple turnovers, and biscuits. Maggie brought a basket as well, and between the two of them there was plenty to eat. While the girls got the meal ready, Ramy and Dewey walked along the water. When it was time, Maggie called them back.

Dewey sat down by Ophelia and gave her a beautiful bouquet of flowers. No boy had ever given her anything in her life. She blushed and looked up at him with a smile. That's when he took her hand.

"Filia, I sure do like spending time with you a whole lot. You are a fine cook and so sweet. I am saving all my money to build a house. Can I ask your Pa for permission to court you?"

Ophelia didn't quite know what to say, so she smiled as big as the sky and nodded yes.

Ramy and Maggie clapped their hands, and it seemed like everyone was talking at once. Dewey promised not to leave it for long. He would talk to Ramsey as soon as they returned to the Youngblood farm.

Ophelia knew she was young, but she was already a year older than Ma was when she got married. And Dewey had a good job and was a church going man. She had no doubts that Papa would say yes. Dewey reached over and tugged one of the green ribbons from a braid in her jet-black hair. He winked at her as he tucked it into his breast pocket. Ophelia quickly looked to Maggie who nodded reassuringly. Ophelia's heart was in her throat. What a strange and wild feeling came with this Irish boy.

Tom stood with his back against the shaded side of the depot. This was the second Saturday in a row that Onni had not made an appearance and Tom was deep in his cups. He had a bead-eye on the sidewalk across the main street. Any sign of the girl or her mother and he was halfcocked and ready to go. It was a personal affront. There may not be a spoken vow, but they had been walking out for over four months now and trading letters. Though her mother might not always be polite about it, Onni hadn't stood him up until now. Something was amiss, and he wouldn't let it stand. He was just as good as any boy from town. He had the Youngblood name. It didn't matter who his pa may have been once upon a time. He was respectable. He worked hard and deserved kindness like any other man. Besides, Onni had shown him favor. Maybe just the once, but after church three weeks ago, they had met in her folks' hay barn and traded more than kisses. Tom loved her. He was sure. And he had told her that he wanted to marry her. They just needed to convince her parents.

These days, he had been working some, running shine for Red. Every buck he made, he put back for himself and Onni. Once he had enough, he knew they could make it out to California. In the West, people didn't care about your color so much. Not religion, either. What mattered is that you could work hard, and the possibilities were endless. With a pretty girl like Onni to love him, well, Tom was just sure there was nothing he couldn't do.

He tipped his hat back and took another sip of Apple Jack. Then he dropped that jar beside the first. Just as he was turning to head back to Red's for more, he spotted her.

Onni seemed to float down Main Street. Her beautiful sky-blue eyes were framed by her golden hair and a grass green bonnet. She tossed her head back and he could hear the music of her laugh. Lord, he loved it when she laughed. He felt it in his feet, and it rolled up his gut until his stomach was in his throat. He couldn't help the smile that spread across his face. He started across the way and then he stopped cold. He heard a yell and jumped back just in time to miss getting killed dead by a team of sorrel trotters pulling a wagon. But he didn't take his eyes off what had paralyzed him in the first place.

Onni's hand was resting delicately in the crook of Otis Travers' elbow. And it was the whisperings of this same Otis Travers that had Onni in peals of laughter.

Tom saw red. Then he saw nothing. But before he could move, Onni saw him. She spun on her heel and quickly dragged Otis back the direction they had come, and they both disappeared. It was over. For that day, at least. Tom slowly came back to himself. And then he did what had sadly become only too familiar. He wandered down to Big Red Harris' shanty on the creek. And he stayed there. For three days.

Ophelia's life was changing fast. Ma and Papa had not only agreed to let Dewey Bailey court her, but they also seemed very pleased with him. He was an industrious man. There was no doubt in that. From dawn on Monday morning until midafternoon Fridays, he was on the tracks. He had started out just pulling and loading cargo, but after a year, he was trained and qualified as an engineer. Ophelia was proud. Especially when Papa explained to her what wits and reflexes and good common sense and a cool head it took to drive a train. He never missed church, and he was good with money. Her brothers liked him, and Tom would too, if he was ever around. Dewey was good with the little ones as well. Most men didn't even hold their own babies, much less someone else's, but it was not a strange sight anymore to catch Dewey singing some Irish song low and sweet with a tired baby on his shoulder after Sunday dinner.

The day he went down on one knee was a day Ophelia would remember for the rest of her life. She would go on decades later to share it not only with her own children, but retelling it for grands, and even great grands. It was March and there was not a cloud in the sky. It was early on a Friday evening, and Dewey hadn't even been home a whole hour when he showed up asking if Ophelia could go walking. Ma stuck her head out the door when Ophelia called,

"Ma, can someone come walking? Dewey's home and chores are done. Just for a bit?"

Delphi considered carefully. Ophelia watched her with wide anxious eyes. Ma was always quiet and thoughtful. Even more so lately. She couldn't use her arm anymore, the one on the side with the sore and the knot. For so long she had treated it with poultices and ointment, but now it hurt enough and often enough that she would sometimes take the opium that the doctor had left for her. Ophelia helped her change the bandages, and she knew how bad it must be. It was an ulcer the size of a chicken egg, and it smelled something fierce. Ophelia tried to help as much as she could and would only go with Dewey when chores were managed.

"Ya'll are alright. Just behave," Delphi whispered.

Ophelia looked at her in shock. No chaperon?

"Ma, you alright? Do you need me to stay?"

Delphi just laughed and shooed them outdoors.

Dewey took up Ophelia's hand and headed across the dirt road and into the woods that headed toward Ox and Pat's cabin. There were tiny little flowers poking through the moss on the forest floor. Dewey talked as they went along, and Ophelia occasionally bent over and picked a bloom.

Dewey was telling her about important things. He had so many plans. He was smart. Sharp as a tack and always thinking. Today he told her that he had finally saved enough for a home. And he had been making plans for building for months. But then a few weeks back, he bumped into Mr. McNair. They were both downtown and fell into talking about how things were growing so quick in Alpena Pass. Travelers were coming in and visiting. But some were staying. Mr. McNair had a big house in town and also owned the feed lot, one of the stores, and the older of the two hotels that lined main street. He was investing in the railroad and his fields out North of town. He was going to put up shot gun housing to keep up with all the newcomers. And he was thinking of letting some of his commercial real estate go to finance the clapboard houses that would be built.

Ophelia was listening intently. Dewey's mind was fascinating and everything he said, well, he turned it into a story. She loved to listen to him talk and watch him recount his adventures. His words painted pictures and his smile was like sunshine. And he wore it almost all the time. Many people in town had nicknamed him Happy, just for this reason.

Dewey stopped walking. He turned to Ophelia and took both her hands.

"Filia, my sweet. I bought the Old Hotel from Mr. McNair yesterday. It has living quarters on the very top. Then the guest rooms. 5 of them. And down below is the restaurant, kitchen, and lobby.

I was thinking, there is no way a body can't make money at a hotel that has a dining room and kitchen in a town growing like a wildfire. What do you think?"

Ophelia DID think. She was quiet for a moment. Then she told him what was in her head.

"Dewey, you're right. And right smart to think of it. Well, folks must stay somewhere, whether they are passing through, or waiting for a house to be ready. Of course, other folks will need to eat as well. Not just the paying guests, so make it an open restaurant. With real down-home food. That will keep your cost low. If it comes with that lot of land behind it, there's room for a garden and chickens. If you grow most of what you serve, it will turn even more money for you. I think it is wise."

She was still turning it over in her head when Dewey dropped to one knee.

"Filia, I don't want to do it without you. I don't really care to do LIFE without you. It was our house money I put up. So, it's OUR hotel. Marry me. Be my wife. Be my partner. I love you, by God, I love you so much my heart's in my mouth!"

Ophelia's mouth dropped open. All she could do was nod her head. Then she went to her knees on the leaves and moss. When they were eye to eye, she surprised herself. She put one hand on Dewey's cheek and kissed him.

That's when he pulled a knotted handkerchief from his pocket. He carefully untied it. There was the most perfect opal sitting atop a beautiful shining gold band. He slowly slipped it on Ophelia's finger.

Then it was his turn. He leaned forward and kissed her soundly.

Tom had been gone awhile this time. Several days. And when he came in, Little Mama was waiting at the kitchen table. She had beans and cornbread sitting on a plate with a mug of good strong coffee. Tom was always careful, but Delphi knew he had become a slave to the bottle. And she was making a stand. It was time to pull the boy back from the brink by his braids, or just to let him go ahead and jump off the cliff if he didn't want saving.

Tom was dirty and bleary eyed. He was wearing the same clothes his ma had last seen him in. And no shoes, but that was typical. The grandparents didn't prefer shoes, and Delphi really didn't either except for town or church. But she kept a wash bucket by the door and used it regularly.

Tom was skinny. Skinny as a wraith. And his eyes were haunted. It brought up the tales of the wendigos that Ox and David used to scare her with as a child.

Neither Tom nor his ma said a word, but their eyes met, and he pushed his long hair back and sat down in the chair. He ate ravenously, like a stray dog, but he kept his eyes on Little Mama.

"Well?" Delphi leaned back and gingerly crossed her arms over her chest. Her eyes were unblinking and hard.

Tom swallowed and fished for words. He swallowed again and took a drink of coffee stalling for time.

They continued to stare at one another. Then Delphi tried a different track.

"Does she have a name?"

"Onni Gerritsen." Tom allowed.

Delphi pressed on. And Tom began to piece the story out for his ma, bit by painful bit. By the time he got to Otis Travers, Tom had stopped eating and looked like he was in physical pain.

Delphi ached to touch his shoulder, but she knew he wouldn't tolerate that. Instead, she told him the truth, as hard as it was.

"They're white, Thomas. And Lutheran. They won't budge. The world isn't ready. I know Papa and I broke the rules with our marriage, but these are foreigners. Rich folks from somewhere else. And those walls aren't coming down any time soon. If she's walking out with Mr. Travers, I'm bound she's engaged, and that means it's as good as done. Find a girl from the county. Or travel to the rez. There're also a few fine Cherokee families in Carroll County as well. But, Tom, oh Tom. She's not for you."

At that, Tom's eyes clouded over, he shoved back his chair, put his hat on low over his eyes and left the house.

It was a Tuesday, and Ophelia was at Iko Neosha's house. Usually during the week, she stayed home, helping Ma with the little ones and doing the housework. No one made any secret anymore that Ma was sick. Delphi did all she could and reigned like a queen and led like a general, but when it came to the actual foot work, Ophelia was the key soldier. But with the wedding coming up and the hotel business looming large, time with Granny was essential.

Long ago, Neosha had sat with Delphi and Jetty at her side and named off plants and roots. She had helped them memorize prayers and rhymes that told the tales of the power of Creator's handy work and all that it was good for. Or bad for. Whatever the case may be. It wasn't magic, but a special talent and knowledge passed down from woman to woman in a line stretching back more generations than a person could count on two hands. Knowledge of the moon and stars, the seasons, how to heal, and how to comfort when healing was not possible. God breathed life into man. He bent over dirt and left some of Himself inside His children. Likewise, He created everything else, and within each piece of work He left a part of Himself. Once a woman knew which parts of Creator each article contained, then she had received the true gift of Medicine that God wished her to have.

And Ophelia came from a line of powerfully devout Medicine women. Delphi had taught her some, but Granny knew even more. And with Ophelia ready to step out in the world, it was time she improved her education.

Today, as they walked the creek bottom, they each filled a basket. Lavender, rosemary, sage, rabbit tobacco, willow bark, slippery elm, grasses upon grasses, 3 kinds of clay. Ophelia recited the usage and Granny would either nod or supply the omitted knowledge.

Then they talked about the benefits that came with the phases of the moon and what practices flourished or failed under each period.

Ophelia's favorite pieces of information came with the stones and rocks. For there were bits and pieces of the earth in every color of the rainbow. And Creator had instilled them with different gifts He wanted His people to have help along their path. Ophelia always carried quartz and amethyst, jasper and turquoise.

Once they were done with this, they sat down and burned sage while Granny explained how a new house, or hotel in Filia's case, should be swept with salt and sage before moving in while all the floors were still completely bare.

Then they prayed for Delphi's decay and crooned a song of mourning while they discussed a comfort poultice. There were some healings that Creator held back from the People. No one knew why, and it was cause for sorrow.

But it was an honored tradition, and these women took it seriously. If the materials were to be found, it was their responsibility to use what God gave them and help their fellow man.

6

The hotel was large, and Mr. McNair had taken pride in it and kept it in good condition. With the wedding coming up, time was pressed, but Filia and Dewey were still using every spare minute to prepare for their move and the new business. They had been lucky and Filia had been right. The nice sized lot behind the hotel was part of the purchase and it was plenty big enough for a vegetable garden and a hen house and flock pen. Ma was setting her a clutch and Pa was happy to make a wedding gift of any seed the couple wanted.

Filia had already planted oregano for croup, ginger for flu, basil, garlic and elderberry for colds and infection. The vegetables and flowers would source the kitchen and decorate the rooms.

Between cutting patterns and sewing with Maggie and Ma, Filia had made time to ferry Granny into town in the wagon and they had sprinkled sage and salt over all three stories of floors and the attic, then swept corner to corner of the hardwood with a dried cinnamon straw broom. They also smudged attic to basement and planted rosemary by every doorway. Once the furniture was out, dusted, and moved back in, a small piece of white quartz was placed under the head of every bed. And a Bible placed in every room. There was no point in doing anything at all unless you set out to do it the right way.

Dewey was working even harder than usual on the railroad. It seemed like they were seeing less and less of each other as their marriage drew near. But Ophelia knew he was taking extra shifts and longer hauls to earn extra in anticipation of their life together.

Soon the time would come when the lodging part of the hotel was ready. Then Filia could focus on the top floor and the living quarters. And after that, the wedding day itself. It was just a single day, and her marriage to Dewey Bailey was a lifetime. Yet she was still excited at the thought of the celebration itself and an opportunity to feel special and present herself to her husband.

But there were worries that came unbidden, especially when she lay in her bed at night in the room she shared with her little sisters Bonnie and Nesa. After the twins were born, Ma had no more children. In a painful blessing, the Lord had seen that her birthing days were over. None of the babies were truly babies anymore. Ats and Nesa were almost 4 and out of diapers. Bonnie, the only other daughter, and true female consolation to their mother, was 7 and plenty old enough to shoulder some of the load. Ophelia had been quite the hand by that age. All the boys were older and took a huge chunk of chores off Pa's plate. And Papa was good to spread them towards Ma's chore list as well. They had grown up knowing 'work', not woman's work or man's work. Just the teamwork it took to run a family and a farm. Just the way Ramy and Little Joe had taken turns between the house and field when Ophelia was smaller, and Ma was always big in the belly with one baby or another. But now, as the oldest girl, Ophelia worried about her mother. Delphi NEVER complained. But she was obviously in great pain. She was tiny from the start, but no amount of food ever increased her girth, and she often had to rest in her weakness. Her bad arm was useless. No one ever said a word, but as the one who dressed and cared for the wound, Ophelia knew it had gone sour. At first it wept. Then she had noticed the smell when she changed the bandages and washed it and applied the poultice. But as the years had gone on, Filia began to notice it when she walked in the room. And then, when she had been to visit somewhere, she could sense it when she re-entered the yard. It was no longer a sore, nor an ulcer. It was a hole, and it had eaten through to her mother's insides. Ma would join Creator. Sooner than later. And here, Filia was in love with Dewey and preparing to leave and start her own home. How could she leave? Who would mother the little ones?

Soon enough it was the day before Filia would stand at the alter and take Dewey's name. She found herself in her Ma's kitchen with all the women in the family. Her aunties, Miriam and Pat were finishing the cake they would celebrate with after church tomorrow. Her sister-in-law Maggie was on her knees hemming up the wedding dress Filia wore, and Ma and Granny Neosha sat by the window dealing out stories and advice on babies and men and all manner of wifely knowledge. It seemed a gay picture of feminine bliss that might have harkened back to any period since the dawn of time. A tribe of women handing down tradition on the eve of a great ceremony. But suddenly, Filia burst into tears.

The room went dead silent except for the sobs of the young bride. Delphi rose from her rocker and crossed the room to gently put one arm around her oldest daughter.

"Sweet, are you afraid?"

Ophelia sniffed and stopped her weeping. She took a deep breath and decided to just out with it. There would never be a better moment or a more appropriate time.

"Ma, what will you do when I go?"

The women looked one to another. They all gently smiled and came together in the center of the room in an embrace.

Maggie spoke first.

"Filia, I can see this house from my front porch. I can hear Bonnie laugh when she wakes up in the morning."

Next Iko Neosha spoke in her deep quiet voice.

"I have known your mother's thoughts and heart since she first kicked in my womb. I often know when she is sick before SHE does."

Then Delphi put her hand under Ophelia's chin and raised her beloved girl's face to look straight into her eyes.

"I have raised you to move on and mother the next line of our People. And you will do it well. Do you not know that we are all tied by the cord of Life? Creator will never separate us. We are each links in a chain that began before Red Elk parted the waters. The little ones grow every day. They are links too. If you do not move on, how will they grow up and follow you? It is your job to go."

Ophelia dried her eyes. They were right. She had to have faith. Everything had a season. And this was the season of her beginning. She would manage it with grace and strength. And she would make her mother proud. For if the world could look at Ophelia and see Delphi and Neosha, then she would know she was doing something right.

Papa had walked her down the aisle to the alter where Dewey and Preacher Thomas were waiting. The whole family was there to wish them well. Even Tom had slipped into the church door and sat in the back pew at the last minute. He was unwashed and smelled of moonshine with bloodshot eyes and tangled hair. But he was there. It broke Ophelia's heart and eased her worry a bit at the same time.

The words were said, and Ophelia had her kiss. Those clear ocean eyes never left hers and she felt she could look into them forever. Dewey treated her like a queen and included her in his every thought. He was depending on her heavily to make a go of the hotel and café. He would keep working the railroad for the time being until their business was independent enough to stand alone. He was just so smart. And he told Filia she was smart too. And he made her believe it.

After the celebration, they loaded up in Dewey's wagon and headed towards Alpena Pass. He had two beautiful small grey mares. Doe and Lily. They had kind soft eyes and were gentle enough for Filia to drive them herself if she desired. That was nice. It meant that she could make trips to the farm while her husband was away on the tracks during the week. She would feel better if she could check on Ma.

Before they left, she had pulled Tom aside. She had a special favor to ask. She wanted to count on him to come visit her. To bring her news and reports of Ma and Pa and how the little ones were behaving so she could come when she was needed. But Tom would not look her in the eye. And he only grunted in answer to her request. His breath was hard and foul. This was not her Thomas. This was not her other-half-soul-brother. He had been changing so much over the past year. And all that was left was anger and bitterness. If bile could be a person, it would be this hard cold young man standing before her. A single tear slipped down her face. She reached up and patted his cheek anyway and turned and walked away from him before he could turn his back on her.

But that had been the only sad part of the day. Her family waved as she and Dewey drove off to the hotel to settle in as husband and wife.

At 13 Seth like to think himself a man. And with Will and Sam following him around in hero worship, it was easy to imagine it was true. All three boys had their Ma's black Osage eyes and the soft sandy Youngblood curls. They were tall and lean like their father and older brothers. They were generally well behaved but could work up quite the ruckus once chores were done and they were turned to their own devices to run wild about the farm and creek banks.

Their favorite pastime was to try to scout Tom. Tom was a brave. They were not quite sure how that made him different from them, but it was very exciting and seemed dangerous. Tom was quiet and seemed to always have a secret. He never ever spoke. And he carried a knife in his boot. He could kill a deer or a rabbit or a squirrel with that knife. Just sneak up on it and-whip-the critter was dead. Then he brought it to Ma to cook. Tom spent some time in town, and some in the field. But he had a special friendship with his Agiduda Atsadi. Tom and Grampy both had long black braids like Ma and Filia and Granny. And Tom and Grampy didn't grow beards. They were real Indians.

Sometimes, with Seth in the lead they could follow Tom almost all the way to the crossroads near the railroad tracks. But they always lost him there. Tom didn't leave footprints or any sign at all. No broken grass or twigs. It was frustrating. He was older, so Seth hoped and prayed that maybe when he and the little boys grew more that they would get better at tracking, too. At least they never got caught. Tom was prickly. He would be mad and might even thrash them if he saw them tailing him. Seth was constantly reminding Will and Sam to stay low and silent. It was a perpetual fear that Tom would find out and there would be fire to pay.

And then one lucky special day, Sam and Will got caught inside practicing their ciphers. Seth was done in the garden and allowed to go out alone. It was just what he had been waiting for. He knew that if he didn't have his little brothers dragging behind, he stood a chance of keeping up with Tom.

Of course, since it was past noon, Tom had a jump on him. But Seth knew where to start. Once he made it to the depot, he stayed out of sight, and sure enough, there sat the older boy, on a salt barrel, mason jar to his lips, hat tipped back, staring at the wooden walk across the street.

Seth hunkered down beside some crates and stared across the street too. He had no earthly idea what they were looking at. But he sat, squat down for what seemed like hours and Tom never moved until his jar was empty. Then he dropped it beside the barrel and opened a second. The people in town moved back and forth in front of the stores and crossed the street. The afternoon passed, and Seth still couldn't make hide not hair of what was so blasted interesting. Then, just before it was getting time to head home or be late for supper, Tom suddenly jumped to his feet.

It happened so fast; Seth fell back on his bottom. Tom yelled out a word that Seth had never heard before, but the way it spat from Tom's mouth, Seth knew he best never repeat it. Then in one swift motion, the older boy pulled the sharp knife from his boot and whipped it halfway across the road where it landed tip down and stuck in the dirt. A man on the sidewalk was staring at

Tom. He had heard the dirty word and he had seen the throw of the knife. Tom strutted out into the street, pulled his blade from the ground and walked toward the creek.

Seth ran all the way home.

Delphi sat at the kitchen table. Bonnie stood beside her.

"Nicely done, Bonbon. The biscuit dough is even and all the same thickness. About as deep as your thumb when laid on its side. Now go get the little jelly jar and start cutting them out."

Bonnie did as she was told, dusting flour off her hands onto her apron as she went. She was a quick learner and took pride in all she was being taught. Helping Little Mama was a pleasure. It came with encouragement and many compliments. Somehow, Ma always made it feel like a game and she always bragged to Pa as well when he came in from the fields. That was her parents' way, constant positive reinforcement. And it worked well. They turned out willing, hardworking, competent young citizens.

Right at this moment Ats and Nesa were out back gathering eggs and feeding the chickens. They were not quiet like some of their siblings, but they did not fear the rooster and hardly ever dropped an egg. Everyone had a part to play and there was a chore to fit every age and stage of childhood. Lessons were the stuff of life and nonstop learning made for successful adults.

Delphi's life was always busy, but she found time for prayer. More and more as she matured. Childhood seemed such a long time ago, and the last 16 years had flown by. She never would have guessed on that fateful June day when she was 14 that she would be sitting here surrounded by such a big happy family of her own. Nor would she have guessed that she would be preparing to leave them all so soon. She would have hoped for a lifetime more with Ramsey, and watching her children grow, and holding grandbabies of her own. The violence brought on her as a young girl had not broken her. Losing her sister, and her own babies had not killed her. Even this pain she lived with every minute of every day was not ripping her life away. But the cause for it could not be denied and it could not be waylaid forever. She had known when her milk did not come in for the twins that it was cancer. And she also knew that there was nothing that could be done about that. She had only hoped that it would have eaten away more slowly, so that she could count her minutes a little longer. But instead, she focused on giving lessons and trying hard to make memories, especially with the youngest of her brood. For some of the children were still so small that she might leave them before she made much of an impression at all. And that was truly her only fear.

7

There was a lovely large sign over the front door and windows of the hotel and café. In copperplate gilt it declared Bailey Hotel est. 1916.

Ophelia was so proud. This was just for her and her husband. If it did splendidly, well that was their success. And if it went down in flames, that was their failure just the same. But it would not fail. The chickens were thriving, the garden was flourishing, and her kitchen already had a name for itself. All three meals saw the dining room packed. And most weekends every boarding room was booked. On top of that, they had 2 semi-permanent boarders. A pin-straight teacher lady and a bachelor working in the bank. He was very well behaved and said he would be with them until time and money saw his house built in Mr. McNair's development just beyond town.

So, when Dewey was gone on the railroad, off making adventures and steady money, Filia was not truly alone. And much too busy to get lonely. She drove out every Wednesday afternoon between lunch and dusk to check on her folks. And she always made it to Denver Church on Sunday with Dewey beside her. Marriage suited them both very well. Though Filia had a queer feeling that their union was a bit different, maybe even more modern that the relationships she was accustomed to.

They told each other everything. There were no secrets, and no embarrassment. There was no shame. All her life, Filia had grown up with female talk, and man's talk. Just like that last day home, in the kitchen with all her aunties, sister-in-law, Ma and Granny. Lectures and instructions on the hushed side of a wifely life. Ophelia had always understood the mechanics since she grew up on a farm. Lordy, she had even helped bring Bonnie, Ats, and Nesa into the world. But the little whispers that only a married woman shared with another wife-those were special. Filia was sure Granny or Ma would faint dead away if they knew how she and Dewey talked.

For instance, Granny Neosha had pulled Filia aside the very next day after Dewey had asked Papa for Filia's hand. They had walked long and far away from the house, out into the woods and then sat side by side under a large oak tree. Granny took Filia's hand and placed a palm sized brown envelope into it.

"Child, the People love babies. The Earth provides for us, and in return we give back babies so that the old ways never die. But men sometimes will want to make a baby on you when your body is sick. Or when the crops are poor. Or the weather is hard. So, it has always been. Mother Moon has given women wisdom for this bringing of babies. Father Sun has passed different wisdom to our men.

"In this envelope is tea. Enough for a pinch in your cup once a day for three months. This is a good start. Begin gathering the herbs to restore your supply immediately. Always, every day, drink one cup of this tea. Made and brewed with a single pinch. Then, when you are ready to become a mother, stop drinking your tea. In 3 moons, your husband's baby will grow inside you. After the child is weaned, start drinking the tea again until you wish for another baby. See? Husband does not have to know. This is woman's work."

Ophelia gazed at her Granny with wide suspicious eyes. This was not a medicine they had discussed before. This was not exactly healing. It felt different. She continued to look at Granny, slowly opening the package and began to smell the contents piece by piece.

Then she spoke,

"I can make out some of this, Granny. Do say, what is it?

"Blossoms of Queen Anne, Primrose crushed into pulp, shaved Lily Root. An abundance of Juniper and dried Indian Paintbrush. The Paintbrush. That is why you must always be gathering. You know you will not find it easily or at all times of the year."

Filia arched an eyebrow. That was the look that showed her kinship to Uncle Ox.

"And it will do no harm? I have heard…."

Neosha put a steadying hand on Filia's face.

"Paintbrush and Primrose. Yes, yes, I know. And this would bring the wrath of Creator, for as we said early on, the People love babies. So, must Creator. If a child has taken root, then yes, large amounts of Primrose pulp and Paintbrush will wash the child away. But if taken in a tiny pinch of tea BEFORE quickening, then Creator will not allow a child to start.

"Never start a child when your man must go away. Never start a child that will come in coldest winter. Never start a child when other children are already hungry. And do not bring a child before your youngest is out of diapers. You will live a stronger happier life. It is so."

Not only had Granny made sure this secret was given in private, but that not even the other women heard. Filia thought it strange then, that Ma had so very many children, if tea was such a simple solution. But that was Ma's lookout, and Filia asked no questions.

So Filia was very sure she was not supposed to talk of this with anyone. But that was not the kind of bond she and Dewey shared.

The first night, as they arrived in the wagon at The Bailey Hotel, Dewey reined Doe and Lily around to the lot behind the building. There was a fine horse shed for them. The couple worked together to curry them down and make sure they had feed and water. Then they penned up the chickens, gathered eggs, and entered their home through the back-kitchen door. Dewey, ever the romantic goose, swept Filia up in his arms and crossed the doorstep before setting her down on the tiled floor. Then he locked it behind them. With a shout, worthy of a schoolchild on chore money day, he raced up the stairs, hollering,

"Bet I can beat cha!"

Filia was stunned for a moment, then took to the chase like a pro. Once halfway up the steps, she grabbed Dewey by the ankle and yanked him backwards, using his fallen body to climb to the top. She cornered the turn in the hall like a racehorse jockey and when she got to their room, she clambered on the bed.

That is where Dewey found her, jumping up and down arms outstretched, bellowing,

"I win, I win, I win, where's my biscuit? I win!"

And with that, Dewey grabbed her about the waist and toppled her onto the quilt covering the bed. Through her giggles, he began to kiss her quite passionately. And that is when the mood changed. Filia realized that she did not want to begin this miracle of a life with this angel of a husband on a lie.

"Happy?" She loved the nickname and it stuck, "After you asked for my hand, Granny and I had many talks."

Dewey lay on his side before her and played with her inky braids.

"Mother Moon passes medicine on to my People."

Dewey answered her with even tone, and rapt attention,

"Like the rosemary by the doors, and the salt sweeping? I understand. We have our ways back home, and I will even tell you about the Little People someday."

"Yes, very much like that Happy. But there is also some ancient private medicine that we are not supposed to talk about or share among Others. But this is about you too, not just me. And I won't have secrets."

Dewey was enthralled now. He was sitting up straight, looking at Ophelia with curiosity. She got up from the bed and went to her chest. She pulled out the brown envelope. Then with a blush, she held it out to her husband, warning him not to spill the contents.

She explained about the restrictions Mother Moon had passed on to all the ancient mothers. And about why it was important to have babies only when a woman felt safe, fed, and at peace. She told him about spacing births to protect the mother's health and to make sure each child got important bonding and lesson time with the parents. Then she told him about drinking the tea every day and how she truly wanted his agreement, but she just felt it so unwise to start a baby until the hotel was sound and Dewey was off the tracks.

Dewey had listened carefully and expressionlessly to the entire practical explanation. He gave the envelope back and then he rose off the bed.

He went to the chest of drawers where he kept most of his clothes and personal belongings. He came back to the bed with a slightly smaller envelope made of vellum. Then he took Filia's hand again. This time he was smiling ear to ear, looking as though a cat had eaten a canary.

"I won't infringe on your female sensitivity by asking if you want a look, but these here, Sweet, are something the French and the Navy boys use. There is no way I am leaving you for a week at a time, here, with all this hotel and café to run, no man at your side, and then adding a big belly and a baby to the mix. So, you go, drink your tea. I'll deal with the French, my darling. And when you get back, we shall conquer the world."

Ophelia pitter pattered to the kitchen, proved indeed that a watched pot never boils, and finally gulped down her tea.

Then she skipped along to the stairway and mounted the steps twice as fast as when she had raced Dewey.

The sun was sinking in the sky, and Filia had just made it back from the farm. Bonnie was helping as much as she could. Granny Neosha was coming every day now to help change bandages and fix meals. Ma was sleeping a lot. The laudanum and opium that the doctor had prescribed had gone from something Ma would not touch into something she needed just to sit up in her rocker for a while and read the bible to her children.

These visits were sad and worrying. This time, Ophelia had slipped out a little early and walked to the field to see Papa. He looked so much older.

She approached the subject delicately,

"Papa, is there anything you need?"

Ramsey had pulled her close and laid his cheek on the top of her head.

"You look and sound so much like Little Mama."

"Papa, when time is small, call for me?"

Ramsey let go and stepped back, wiping his face with his kerchief. He nodded and turned quickly away, back to work.

Filia thought all this over now, back at the hotel, while she swept the front walk. Supper was on the stove and customers and boarders would soon make their way into the dining room.

That's when she saw him. It was Tom. He was straight across the street. He sat atop a barrel outside the depot, a mason jar to his lips. His hat was pulled low, and she could not see his eyes. And my, she was angry. She had not seen him since she moved to town with Dewey two months ago. She leaned the broom against the doorstep and marched out into the street.

Before Filia made it halfway across the dirt, Tom jumped up and yelled a foul, filthy word. His eyes were trained past Ophelia and a bit to the right. She turned. It was Otis Travers, and he was walking with a blonde woman, big in the belly. It looked as though they might be headed into Filia's very own café. She looked back at Tom. He was still yelling and pointing. He stumbled into the street and then he fell on his face. Filia stood frozen. She had no idea what to do. And then suddenly, Otis Travers was rushing past her. He ran right up to Tom and kicked him in the side and spit on the ground beside him. Otis' face was purple with rage.

"You'll answer for this, Youngblood," then he turned to rejoin the pregnant woman on the sidewalk.

Filia went to Tom and kneeled beside him.

"C'mon, Tom. Let me feed you."

Tom rolled up onto his feet and ran towards the creek. Filia stood up, brushed her apron clean, and crossed back over the street to wait on her customers.

When Dewey made it home that next Friday, Filia was waiting for him. She welcomed him home with a kiss and fed him well. She sat quietly and listened to all the places he had been and all he had seen. When he was out of stories, she was still silent.

"Filia, love. What's wrong, is it your Ma?"

Filia shook her head, then she got straight to the point. She told her husband about the humiliating scene she had witnessed. And the information she had gathered simply by waiting on the tables in her café. Otis Travers had married Onni Gerritsen months and months ago. And there was distasteful scuttlebutt that her baby was well on its way before the vows were said. She now knew that when Tom had disappeared, he had vanished into his moonshine and kept company on the creekbank with bootleggers and other dangerous men, criminals. And that he stayed drunk and mad.

The people in town said that right up until the very day that the French girl married, it had appeared very much as though she and Tom were an item. And that is where the gossip stopped. At least that is where the folks stopped chattering when they saw

Tom's sister was close enough to hear. But the implications were enough. The whole town was on tenterhooks, waiting to see what color the baby would turn out to be.

Dewey put his face in his hands. He knew much of Tom but had hardly spoken two words to the young man in all the time he had known him. He was troubled, and Dewey knew about fights and other dirty tales, not meant for a woman's ears. Especially his sweet Filia's. But they all led to the same verdict. Tom was a sot. A broken-hearted drunk. Dewey promised to ride over and see Ramy tomorrow and figure something out.

When Dewey returned to Alpena Pass on Saturday afternoon with Ramy in tow, it was not hard to find Tom. He was perched like a gargoyle on his salt barrel sipping on his mason jar. Two empties littered the ground beside his post. Dewey and Ramy walked over and leaned against the side of the depot silently. Tom had his hat pulled low and did not look up. They all gazed blindly across the street to the stores and the café. After quite a little bit, Tom spit out harsh words,

"Ain't going home. Try. Just try to make me."

At that, Dewey and Ramy sprang into action, they jumped up and each grabbed one of Tom's arms. They dragged him, kicking and screaming down to the creek and dunked him multiple times. Once he finally gave up and the fight was clean out of him, they let him go. He sputtered and floundered until he found his feet.

"I ought a cut ya both. What the hell, boys?"

And Ramy began to speak. He talked about family and pride and women. And then he got to Little Mama.

"Tom, not being there, not seeing it don't mean it ain't happening. She's slipping away and soon. And she cries for you every damn day, son. Get your boots home. Whatever meanness you need to work out can wait until Little Mama's gone and can't see it."

Tom hung his head. Then he wrung his hat out as all three of them headed home.

Ma didn't look like she was long for the world. But Sunday was Sunday. And the family had all been in church, filling the better part of three pews. Little Mama smiled so wide her face might crack right in two. Joe Joe was home for a visit and full to the brim with tales of the Wild West. They were all gathered at the Youngblood farm for the afternoon. Filia, Pat, Miriam, and Maggie worked in the kitchen, preparing the meal. The men wandered here and there, visiting and talking of work, and live-stock while the children ran and laughed. Tom was there, too. His 'baptism' had done him some good. He was sitting on the porch beside Little Mama's rocker listening to her whisper light voice. It made her eyes shine.

Little Bonnie was trying hard to help the ladies in the kitchen. Filia gave her sister a hug and told her to go play. She would not have many more chances to just be a child and they all knew it. Filia wanted her to have the time she could.

The youngest of the cousins joined Ats and Nesa chasing chickens and wreaking havoc in their wake. It was a beautiful sight to behold. A wonderful mix of brown and white skin, blonde, brown, red and raven hair. Eyes in all shades. And they were a family. Some came in the natural way, and some from what might be called tragedy. But Little Mama always said, Beauty from Ashes. God had given her more love than anything He had ever taken away.

Once the food was done, the men were fed, then the children. Only after that did the women settle on the porch. Ophelia claimed pride of place and sat beside her mother and helped her eat. Delphi was skin and bones. Her pain pulled her face, but she still never mentioned it and always had a smile for those she loved. She reached over and patted Filia's head.

"I wish I could see you be a mama. But you'll see to it when the time is right. Don't let the little ones forget the People, Ophelia."

"No, Ma. Nor Red Elk, or Creator. I promise."

At that, Delphi looked up. Ramsey was leaning against the porch rail, staring at his wife. His whole heart was in his eyes.

Delphi smiled just for him and let her head lay on the back of the chair.

"Husband, I'm tired now, I believe I will go to bed."

Ramsey walked over and picked her up. She was light as a child. Without thought, he kissed the top of her head and went in the house to take her upstairs.

The day they buried Delphinium Alice Little Hawk Youngblood it drizzled all day. But somehow, that seemed fitting.

Delphi had been the sun in their lives. The family alone made a crowd in the burying yard. But there were folks from Denver and the church. There were people from town and friends from other communities. Many had liked and respected her. Everyone had turned out to pay tribute. There were too many flowers to count, and they made the small grave look even tinier than it was. Only one face was missing. Tom was nowhere to be found.

Delphi had been so young. 31 years old. She had borne more pain in her short life than was fair. But she had also created so much joy. She had ten living children to number the beats of her heart. And Esther and a tiny baby boy were awaiting her at Heaven's gate. She would finally meet with Jetty again. And her husband Ramsey would mourn her all of his days. She had raised his orphaned sons, loved him with a fire that burned hot and bright, and given him more happiness than any man deserved. She had never shown anything but love. And though she moved through life like a quiet breeze, she had left an enormous impact.

Neosha and Atsadi were broken. A parent should not out-live a child, let alone two. But they had many grandchildren and two grown sons to propel them on towards the future. They knew they were needed now, more than ever before. And they were relieved that their daughter was finally out of pain.

Dewey held Ophelia and she cried into his shoulder. She would have given anything for more time with her Ma. But well and truly Ma had taught her so very many things. It was Filia's job to remember them and pass them on, not only to her own children, but to her sisters as well.

Delphi had come into the world so gracefully. Almost on tiptoe. Her wide eyes had taken in everything around her without judgement or question. She was always at task and always lending help. And she was wise beyond her years. Neosha could not help but remember the words Delphi had spoken so certainly the night before she married Ramsey when she was still just a child,

"Lots of times Ma, it is better to just BE, instead of ponder. Most questions answer themselves if you watch and listen to everything going on around. And if there is still a question, then I listen harder, so I can hear God."

Delphi had always been listening for God. And now, she was with Him.

Life would never be the same, but it would go on. In these last few months, all anyone had wanted was peace for Little Mama. And that was what she had now. Even Tom and Joe had gathered to the farm in the end. Delphi had gone to bed after a happy Sunday, full of her favorite people and her most treasured moments. Then she had slipped off and simply not woken up. No one could wish for an easier passing.

But as is so often the case, sorrow and hard times were left for those who remained. Uncle David and Aunt Miriam took in the twins, Ats and Nesa. They only had one son, Robert, then God had blessed them with no more. They had plenty of room and plenty of love. And the twins were the youngest and would need the most care.

That left Bonnie at home with her passel of brothers, and her the only girl. Papa was downtrodden, but he pushed on. The boys helped with the chores and Bonnie was proud to keep house and look after the menfolk. Ophelia and Dewey came whenever they could to make sure all ran smoothly, and they helped where they could.

Granny spent much of her time at the Youngblood farm helping Bonnie. She was taking the time to contribute to the younger girl's education. Whenever Ophelia visited, Bonnie was overflowing with what she was learning. They talked of herbs and healing, Red Elk and moon phases. Filia enjoyed remembering her own early days and the enthusiasm that came with learning about the People. It was like being part of a giant hoop and finding your place in the circle. Though some of her joy for her sister was darkened by the guilt of not being home to help.

She cherished her time with Happy and truly thrived when in the rush of the hotel and café. Business had taken off. She heard the talk. She knew that she kept the cleanest establishment in town and that her cooking was also deemed the best to be had for a good price, too. She now knew all her neighbors downtown, the people who lived behind or above their businesses. The man who owned the Mercantile, Mr. Keys, had a daughter the same age as Filia. Agnes was courting, but not married yet, and the girls spent much time together when Happy was on the railroad. The girls would sit and crochet, or sing together, or tell tales. Agnes had a little terrier dog. It was the sweetest thing. And Ophelia thought she just might ask her husband for a pup. It might make her time without him less lonely, and her waiting for a baby more tolerable. There were days Filia wished she could skip her tea, but she knew that their plan was smart and sound. Still, it didn't change her longing.

Her friendship with Agnes Keys was a balm for her soul. It helped just a wee bit to fill the hole that had been left when Ma had passed from the world. They had met just at the right time. Ophelia was even able to confide in Agnes about Tom. She told of his story from beginning to end. And Agnes confessed that she knew most of the facts. And had heard the shameful gossip that circulated in Alpena Pass now. Agnes had not seen Tom in weeks either. No one that Filia talked to had any idea where he was. She still loved him dearly. She wanted to find him, move him into the hotel and set him straight. There was many an honest job of work she could put him to. And that might change this path he stumbled down.

But even in her good intentions, her heart strings knew, deep inside where her Spirit lived, that it was already too late.

Atsadi was a shattered man. He loved all his grandchildren the same. But Tom and Ophelia were special. They were fully of the People. They were his pride and his legacy. He was shamed at the way Jetty had been lost to him. And he held no one responsible but himself. He had not been as watchful as he should have been. But People trusted People. And that Mr. Joseph had broken all the bonds. He was *"u so nv i"*. A bad man.

And Tom was cruelly cursed because of it. He would come to a bad end. Atsadi had bonded with the boy and tried to take him under his wing. Especially after the age of 12, when Ramsey could do nothing more with him. Ramsey had tried to be a father to Tom, but there was such resentment built up on the boy's part that a wall had formed.

Now Ophelia, precious Ophelia Winsome. She was a comfort to those around her and such a reminder of her mother. She was a gifted medicine woman. In old days she would have been a Shaman in his Cherokee tribe. And in a way she was, in the tribe they had made here, themselves. She was a bright spot of hope. And he knew she was taking time with little Bonnie to foster the same virtues.

Often now, Atsadi was tired. His back and his jaw hurt when he did his chores. And when he thought back on his losses, or reminisced too hard, there was a tightness in his chest. He knew the meaning of that. But he kept it to himself. He did not need, nor want the doctor. Nor did he go to Neosha or Ophelia. His time was passing, and he would meet Creator with the proud face of a warrior when the time came.

He gave Butter, the lumbering Belgian, an affectionate pat and the apple from his pocket. These days were so different than how he had grown up in Kentucky. But beyond death, both in mortal form, and in the demise of his native lifestyle, there were pleasures left to be had. And today, he would go to the Youngblood farm, herd his grandsons down to the creek, and go fishing.

Filia had never in her life been so glad to have Dewey come home early on a Friday. They were still standing in the back doorway of the Bailey Hotel when they heard loud voices and a gunshot coming from Main Street. Dewey dropped his bag and ran across the width of the building to the front walk. There, he pushed the trailing Ophelia behind him.

Otis Travers was walking straight down the middle of the all but empty street, firing shots into the air and hollering. His face was beet red, and he had lost his hat. His voice was so loud, Filia was sure it could be heard across the county line. And he was bellowing Tom's name.

Ophelia went white. That's when Otis saw Dewey and Filia standing in the doorway. He swung around their direction and mounted the sidewalk. God bless him, he pointed his revolver at the ground. But his words were filled with hate, and he stood so close in front of Dewey that their noses almost touched.

"Best tell me now where that no-good dog is hiding. It'll be better for him if I don't have to search him out."

There was a reason the whole world called Dewey "Happy" instead of Mr. Bailey or Dewey. He had Irish charm and an unusually cool head. Ramy had warned and teased about the temper on Maggie and all Irish. But Ophelia had never seen it. Not on her man. Dewey pushed his hat back, as it was being crushed upwards by Otis' creased forehead.

"Now, Otis," he said good naturedly, "you know we've had a death in the family. My wife is not only standing here, but she is grieving. And you're talking about her own brother. She'll not be hearing words like that from any man on my watch."

"Pardon, Ophelia. But, Happy, you know what all mess he's been up to, and now there's the proof. I can't let it go unchallenged."

Dewey put one hand on Otis' shoulder. And the man stood there and actually let him. Dewey looked at Otis sincerely and spoke slowly.

"It's a sorrow to us, the way he goes about. But you have my word, we haven't seen him since the Sunday before my mother-in-law died. None of us. Not even his family. We've looked. He won't come around, but if he does, I will do my best to send him your way."

Mr. Travers nodded and spun on his heel.

That night after supper was served and cleaned up down in the café, and all the lights were turned out and the doors were locked, Filia still could not sleep. She would close her eyes, but she kept seeing Tom as a small boy. So simple and happy to be chasing rabbits in the grass. And she felt their hearts tied together. It must have been near dawn when she rose.

She went out to their back lot and sat on the hard-swept ground. She placed the few items she had gathered in front of her. There was a small bundle of sage smoldering in a wooden bowl. She placed her good big amethyst stone in the bowl. And she prayed to Creator in Osage, like Neosha had taught her. She hoped that the smoke would carry her prayers to God and that God's protection, secreted in the beautiful purple rock would find its way to Tom and bless him as well.

Then she stood up and went to gather eggs. The sun was coming up, and there was work to do.

Ophelia was beating biscuits and keeping an eye on the bacon. They had a full house this weekend. She was very busy, and she liked it that way. The stacks of paper money that kept gathering were hidden away by Happy in a place not even she knew how to find. That way, if he was gone, no one could come and demand that money from her. She wouldn't even know where to look!

Suddenly an earth-shattering wail broke her early morning silence. Ophelia almost dropped the batter bowl. As she left the kitchen, she nearly ran headlong into Happy who was charging down the stairs pulling up his suspenders. The cry had come from the street. They reached the front door at the same time and Happy flung it open. A jumble of townspeople was standing in a wide grouping around the front door of the hotel.

There, too real to believe, was Tom, lying on his side. One arm was pinned beneath him and the other was flung up in front of his face. He wore no shirt, no hat, and no shoes. Just some dirty pants. There was some blood on the side of the cheek that was facing up. And something sticky on the back of his head in his long beautiful black hair. Ophelia reached down to shake him awake.

Dewey gently grabbed her wrist and pulled her back.

"No, Filia. No. Go to the kitchen."

Ophelia looked at her husband with wide terrified eyes. Happy spoke softly as though to a child,

"Go, Filia, go now."

She did as she was told, as though she was sleepwalking through a horrible dream. Dewey stepped out onto the sidewalk and shut the front door behind him.

He had made haste running to the sheriff. And then the undertaker had been summoned. There were no signs of a fight. And no other wounds. Just the single hole in the back of the head. After the undertaker had done his job and gathered Tom up and took him away, Dewey went next door and asked Agnes to come sit with Filia. He relied on Mr. Keys to sprinkle the sidewalk with some sand. Then he placed the CLOSED sign on the café door. He paused there for a moment, cap in hand with his head bowed. He asked God for strength in the coming days. And to place a hand on his wife.

His little grey team made it quickly out to the Youngblood farm. And the family gathered in dark silence.

Then Atsadi spoke,

"Put him in the ground near Delphi. She was his real Ma. In any way that counted. It's fitting. Braid his hair. But no feathers. And no knife."

His words were firm and final, but his eyes were wet.

By the time Dewey arrived at home, Filia was asleep in their bed. Agnes was in the chair beside her. When Dewey entered the room, Agnes looked up from the bible she was reading,

"I've never…. She just…Oh, Happy. It's like something was torn out of her. I didn't even know a person could hurt like that.

I had Father call the doctor. He gave her something and there is more here on the table if you need to give it to her again later. She made sounds like a wounded animal. She couldn't speak. It was chilling."

Dewey sat on the edge of the bed. He placed his hand in Ophelia's long beautiful hair.

"Thank you so much Agnes. I'll see her through it."

Ophelia was made of tough stuff. She came by it honest, and the whole family was bound to soldier on. Death was one thing, but this was shame as well. They put Tom in the ground that very next day. Just like Atsadi had ordered. No one asked questions, yet everyone could guess what happened. And honestly, Tom was not innocent. He had put himself in the way of a very bad gamble, played dirty, and lost, fair and square.

All that was left to do was to put one foot in front of the other. Or so Ophelia thought. Once the funeral was over, she just got up each day and carried on. She went about her business and waited for this awful time to pass. Those who knew her gave sympathetic smiles and brought pies and flowers. Then there were the reassuring pats on the hand and the offers of prayer. She took it all, for His strength is made greatest in our weakness. Ma had taught her well.

A few days after the horrible events, Ophelia was sitting in the hotel parlor with Agnes between the rush of meals. Happy had wanted to stay home, but Ophelia had sent him on his way. He had work to do, and their dreams should not suffer because Tom had met a bad end. And just like her Ma, she would not dose her life away in sleep if she could avoid it. Filia had practically had to shove him out the door with a kiss to his cheek and a kick to his backside. As the women sat and discussed Agnes' engagement there was a voice from the lobby. Ophelia rose to go see if she had a new boarder.

What she found instead shocked her to the core. It was a woman more than twice her age. She was smartly dressed in tailored clothing, and she carried a bundle wrapped in a fine lace blanket. It was delicate and expensive work. Filia didn't have to finger it, she could tell by looking.

Then the woman spoke, and her words were sharp, the consonants harsh, and the language itself nasal and odd sounding,

"This is the child of Thomas Youngblood. His mother cannot keep him. She has a husband that will want children of his own."

With that, the strange woman thrust out her burden and the minute Ophelia had a good hold on the child, the lady was back out the door.

Ophelia stood there a moment, looking up at the ceiling. All her emotions swirled together and met in a large undefinable nothingness. Then she returned to the parlor. She sat back down beside her friend and took a deep breath. She pushed the beautiful blanket back and revealed wide blue eyes in a dark face framed with black curls. Further inspection proved that Tom had fathered a son. The baby was so fresh and new that the umbilical stump was still attached. He could not have been more than a few days old. That's when he wrinkled up his little face and began to wail.

The girls looked at each other in amazement. Then Agnes jumped to her feet and ran next door to her father's store. When she returned, she was carrying cloth to make diapers, 3 bottles and more material for shifts and blankets.

Once fed and rocked, the tiny dark mite was put to sleep on a pallet in the parlor so Filia could hear him as she went about her hotel chores. Happy wasn't due home until Friday and there was no way to reach him quickly. Filia closed her eyes and said a silent prayer.

So much for plans and Granny Neosha's tea.

By the time Dewey came in on the Friday afternoon train, it was way too late. There was no other course of action they could possibly take other than to raise Tom's baby themselves. Filia had been sleeping with him in the bed beside her so she could hear him in the night. If he was awake, he was held in the crook of her right arm while her left hand did her work. She rocked him and sang him to sleep. She fed him from the bottle, and she was sure she was getting smiles from him when she spoke to him in her sing song Osage language. It was as though all the love she had for Esther and Tom finally had a place to roost. And each wide-eyed smile showed her that her mother-love was definitely returned. All that was left was a name. And she had part of it already. But it couldn't be set in stone until her husband weighed in.

Dewey came in the back door and Ophelia turned to greet him with a kiss. The little boy was front and center, held in her arms like the priceless treasure she deemed him to be. They sat down at the table and Filia spilled out the unbelievable tale. Then she smiled.

"I've been thinking on a name. But, Happy, maybe you would like something Irish?"

"Darling, Bailey is Irish enough. I think he needs something Osage. Something to make him proud and to carry him away from his sorry start."

Ophelia pondered a bit and mumbled to herself....so many sorry starts.

"Nohpazi. It means fearless. Brave. Unafraid. Others can call him Noah. Both ways it fits."

Dewey nodded, firmly in agreement. Then they made plans to set out the next day for the Youngblood farm. They would check with Ramsey, but they were sure all the things from Filia's childhood were still there. The cradle, some clothing, and blankets. And they were sure her Papa would let them have whatever they could find. Then they would introduce Noah to the family.

It was a bright and beautiful morning. There was a smile on Filia's face. And it ran right through to her soul. With the loss of Ma and Tom, such happiness and gaiety were distant memories. She was glad to have a reason to rejoice. Little Nohpazi laughed as the wagon bounced behind the gentle horses. He was holding his head up and cooing whenever spoken to. Filia was sure he was the smartest babe that was ever born. Dewey did not have the disposition to contradict her. It was not what he had expected, nor planned. But his Mam had taught him that God finds a way. And in this instance, though he and his wife had been methodical, it seemed that God's plans were different than theirs. So, Dewey did what Dewey ALWAYS did. He accepted, and he thrived. Perhaps that was why he and Filia were so evenly matched.

When they reached the Youngblood home, Ramsey greeted them in the front yard. He was finding his smile again, but his sorrow was not buried. Then he saw Nohpazi. And with one look into those blue, blue eyes, he was smitten. Grandpa, again. He could move along in this fashion. Here was a happiness handed to him in grief and he grasped it with both hands. Atsadi and Neosha were summoned along with the rest of the large sprawling family. The tiny boy was instantly welcomed and claimed, and the tribe moved on into the next stage of life. No one in the family ever thought to call him anything BUT Nohpazi, though Noah might serve him well as an adult. Time would tell.

Bonnie and Maggie ran to the attic and gathered all the treasured baby things that had defined Delphi's motherhood. And in this way, she was also there. Never forgotten, only just out of reach, a memory in the shadows. Her loss was still new enough to bite and sting, yet at times the feeling she left was a warmth accompanied by a teary smile. These things took time. But her presence was felt on this day.

The beloved cradle crafted so many years ago for Ophelia and Esther was now in the wagon. It would go back to the hotel and be the resting spot for little Nohpazi. How anyone could part with him, Filia could not imagine. Nor how anyone, birth mother or no, could love him more than she did, she would never guess. Happy was proud of him and proud for Filia. He knew he would bond more and differently as the boy grew. That was the way of fathers. Unless someone knew the truth, and many would guess, just by looks, the boy COULD be his son. Obviously, there was a deep resemblance to his beautiful Osage wife. And the blue eyes were not sky clear like Happy's, but the blue could not be denied. (Even if it was a French blue in truth.) No one asked questions so no answers were needed.

But there were other things to sort out. Happy was still six months away from coming off the rails by his and Filia's grand plans. And he didn't cater much to the thought of leaving his wife home for days on end with a newborn. As the women made much over the infant, Happy talked with the men and a plan was hatched.

Seth was very close to his 15th birthday and had been out of school for over a year. He was a good boy. A bit lost without Tom to idolize, but the whole family agreed that was a catastrophe they had come just short of. If given his own room off the larder at the hotel and a regular set of tasks and daily routine, he would do. When Happy offered him $4.00 a week on top of the room and board, Seth was more than willing. He was a hard worker for his Papa on the farm, but anyone could tell that farming was not his passion. He was a little wayward. His attitude was good. He kept to the church and never found any trouble to get into but had spoken of no particular future. Possibly a short stay in town and an opportunity to earn his own money might help him find direction.

Ophelia had plenty for him to do. The garden needed tended, wood brought in, a body could never sweep enough to keep the place clean. And the errands and shopping could be trusted to Seth so she could stay at the hotel tending the business and the baby. In truth, simply having an overgrown boy on the premises made Happy and Filia feel much better about Happy heading back out on the train.

By Sunday afternoon, Seth had gathered up all his belongings and was ready to relocate to town. Sam and Will looked a bit lost, but Papa knew how to keep them busy enough to take their minds off the absence of their older brother. Once in town, Seth was beside himself excited and filled with freedom. The little room in the attic had a cot and shelves and plenty of nails to hang his clothes on. There were only a few barrels of stores he had to share the space with. He felt very grown up. His older sister Filia gave him the balance of Sunday afternoon to explore the town with a warning to stay out of trouble and mind his business. His job would begin Monday morning.

Seth screwed his cap down square on his head and started out towards the north of town. That was the direction he had never been. Out beyond the lumber yard were a few houses and the town school. There were warehouses full of all the things that came and went on the trains. He liked watching them load the trains and imagining where all those bundles and packages were headed. But he wasn't sure he wanted to go very far from the farm when he was grown enough to determine his own life. He started down towards the creek, then he remembered that fateful day he had followed Tom to town. He wasn't sure he understood everything that had happened. But he did know that no good came from the men Tom conspired with down in the shanty community. He thought of his Little Mama, and he turned on his heel and headed back towards main street.

The hotel was impressive when approached from the street like this. The sign was large and neat. The gold lettering caught the eye, and even the sidewalk in front of the building was cleaner than the areas around it. He knew that his sister took great pride in everything she did, and it made him proud too. Filia gave the Baileys and the Youngbloods a fine name, and he knew that reflected on him as well. He came up short with his eyes wide and his mouth open. It was quite the moment of clarity for a teenage boy. The reputation of one's family reflected on the individual. And the inverse was just as true. He ran down his relatives in his head. There was an aunt he never knew, and no one said her name. And then there was Tom. If judged solely on the actions there, a reputation could be ruined with a word. It was unfair. But it could be managed. He must simply think before he acted or spoke. He needed to make sure that when people looked at him, they saw Ramsey and Delphi Youngblood. And now he was in town, everyone would be watching. He realized too, that the actions of family like Filia and Dewey would never echo as far as the one or two bad decisions of a black sheep. The world was not weighted fairly.

8

abies and young men grow quickly. Nohpazi was a strapping, healthy, happy boy. And he always had a smile even if he was quiet as a mouse. He knew Filia for his mama. She was sure, for whenever she came into view, or sang, the babe would widen his eyes and show his gums as he threw back his head and laughed. He was so sweet, and just what Filia needed to comfort her through her grieving.

Seth was taller than she was and growing every day. He ate his own weight in vittles, it seemed, but he worked hard for her. His manners and behavior were impeccable. Filia sometimes had to look twice to make sure it was her own little brother Seth they had taken to board. Such a fine young man, he was always on his dignity. He kept his head down and his nose clean, as Happy liked to put it. And it was such a blessing to have Seth here. By the time Happy came home on Fridays, there was not much left to do.

Filia began to dream of a day when her own home was filled like Little Mama's had been. When it was her pride of place in the pew, her kitchen that was the hub of their little tribe. Happy would soon be home all the time, as his time on the tracks was growing shorter. He was a good father. He was so taken with Nohpazi. And he was guiding Seth with gentle authority. The boy looked up to Happy. His eyes were filled with hero worship all during their weekends. And when Sundays came around, he still shadowed his brother-in-law. Seth sat next to Happy in church, and stood silently by, not quite joining in the men's talk during the family time, but glad to be included.

It was quite a relief that he did not seem to have a heart for young ladies yet. He was shyer than her other brothers had been. He seemed to be much more interested in setting goals and accomplishing them. He listened carefully when instructed on a new task and took great pride in a job well done. He was growing stronger by the day and was content to mark his progress in manual labor.

One afternoon, upon returning from an errand north of town, Seth lingered in the kitchen. Filia was peeling potatoes and preparing for the evening meal. Her garden was growing gang busters. Happy had so many tricks. Between what he had learned from his Irish mother, and what she had been taught from the cradle, they had a veritable Eden right out the back door. She was a wonderful cook, but she had learned some Irish recipes that were a big boon for the café, as well.

Seth didn't make a sound. He watched her awhile. Then he moved over to where the baby was propped in a basket and played absent minded finger games with the child. When he began to hum a tuneless dirge, Filia lay down her knife and wiped her hands on her apron. Then she turned and fixed him in her gaze,

"Well?"

Seth fell silent again and toed the hardwood floor with his boot. Filia sat and waited.

"Sis? You been out past Hill Street lately?"

"Well, let me think. Not in a month or so. When Happy took me out to pick up lumber. Why?"

Seth broke into a smile and his words came quicker now. He was excited,

"All these buildings going up? People are buying lumber, but did you see all the stonework they are doing on that post office? Well, there's a gang of fellas. Irish, I'd take 'em. They sound like Happy. They are out there making a rock yard. Stone yard? I don't know. But I've never seen the like. Wagons coming in, unloading. They're using water and chisels and squaring that rock up, so it lays flat. And then some of them are doing the actual building. It's like a puzzle, that post office. It's clever. It's math, and balance, and...well, Sis, it's like art."

Filia smiled with him.

"Clever art. That sounds interesting Seth. Maybe on Saturday we can take Happy and go see more about it. If they ARE Irish, you bet he knows them. You might could even ask them some questions."

Her brain was already five steps ahead.

Happy and Filia had sat up late Friday night. While he rocked a sleeping Nohpazi, Filia told him everything Seth had said with eyes as bright as her brother's had been. This was an opportunity. This was a vocation. A Godsend.

Happy did indeed know the family of brothers that held the stone masonry at the edge of town. And his own uncle was among their workers. He was quite sure that he could put in a word for Seth and work something out.

Saturday morning, after breakfast was served, Filia had arranged for Agnes to come watch the lobby. The Bailey family loaded up and trotted their greys out towards the bustle on Hill Street. Seth could barely keep still as he ran a nonstop commentary on what he saw.

"...and look there Happy, see that one fella? See how he takes that chisel and mallet? He's taking off all the bumps and points. You know how Agiduda Atsadi knaps his points? It's like that, I figure, but on a much larger scale. And then when they take a load over to the post office, they're gonna lay 'em all even with some mud or daub or something in between. I ain't quite figured that part out yet, and..."

"WHOA, there Seth, breathe," Happy laughed.

A tall broad freckled man approached and threw his hand up in greeting.

"What say, there, Happy?"

Happy shook the man's hand and introduced him as his uncle Seamus Bailey. Seth stepped forward and shook his hand too. The two older men shared a wink. Then the three of them wandered off. Filia sat contentedly on the wagon seat, shading Nohpazi's face from the sun. Before long, she saw Seth pointing and gesturing. Then Happy headed back towards her alone.

On the drive home, Happy was glad to tell her that Seamus would keep Seth busy for the day and then join them for supper. She would lay out a good spread and then her husband could forge their plans. If all went well, by the time Happy was off the railroad, Seth would be on his way to being a mason. Filia was sure that her father Ramsey would be pleased, but they would speak to him tomorrow as well.

Seth would come home tired but thrilled and with a passion for his future in his heart.

Seth had been beside himself with joy when Ramsey gave consent. The boy would spend his Saturdays working under Seamus Bailey learning masonry. It was heavy and precise work. But there was a grand future in it. There were places in the West where trees grew sparsely, and rocks were plenty. Those places needed buildings and towns just like anywhere else. And as Seth had learned and was eager to share, stone was timeless, waterproof and fireproof. Yes, there was going to be money in the stone business.

Seamus and Happy had talked at great length, and it was decided that once Seth could pull a full week's work he would have it at the stone yard. Seamus would teach him the business and help him work his way up. In the meantime, the boy could stay there at the hotel with his sister and brother-in-law and make a life for himself apart from farming. It was what Seth wanted.

In a matter of weeks, Happy would be home for good. They would expand the café hours and put their heart and soul into their hotel. Filia couldn't wait. With her husband's help she could upgrade and change so many things. She kept a running list of ideas. Some things she thought of herself, others came from comments and conversations with her customers. Other ideas came from her dreams. She wanted to jar and put away enough jam and vegetables to sell. She could market her butter and eggs just like her mother had. People could come in, order a meal, and buy pickles to take home. Or a pie. She was busting with lucrative schemes.

Nohpazi was also busting…his first tooth. Filia wasn't fazed by it in the least. She had taken on so much while helping her mother that she knew what to expect and how to cope. A nub of carrot and a finger dipped in whiskey rubbed on his gums did the trick.

Her days were full and happy once again. There was snow on the ground, and the café business was a bit slow, but they had no vacancies in the hotel. Filia and Agnes were spending a quiet afternoon at their mending.

Agnes had married her sweetheart at the end of the spring, and now that Christmas had come and gone, she was bubbling over. The child inside her was beginning to kick. Her cheeks were pink, her smile was ceaseless. Filia could not have been more pleased for her. She loved to lay her hand on Agnes' middle and feel the little thumping movements.

Happy had been home full time for just over three months. It was a blessing. All of their plans were falling into place, and she knew that somewhere, the hidden money was multiplying and building for their future together.

Nohpazi was scooting across the floor and trying to pull up on the furniture. It would not be long until he was toddling about. He babbled and Filia was positive that between the spit and bubbles she was hearing "Ma" very clearly. She was proud of how he was growing. Not all bottle babies fared so well. But her little brother and sister, the twins Ats and Nesa, had done fine, and Filia had expected no less. Still, it would be nice to nurse her own child. She had never paid it any mind until Agnes was expecting. But now she wondered what that might be like. Nohpazi was her flesh and blood. Just the same as Tom had been. And her heart could not have loved him more if she HAD birthed him. Still.

That night, as she and Happy lay in the dark, she reached over and put her hand on his heart and her head on his chest.

"Happy?"

"Mmmmm?" he was almost asleep.

"I'm not going to drink tea anymore…"

"Well then, wife. There's a piece of work to be done."

And with that, he kissed her soundly on the lips.

In the cold hoar frost, Ramsey followed his own footprints back towards the hog pen. He carried heated water and an old shovel. Light or dark, spring or winter, hot or cold, the livestock needed water. And this chore of refilling the troughs and breaking the ice was part of his routine. He had set the boys to other chores first thing, and everyone was doing their part.

Bonnie, in the meantime, was all a bluster in the kitchen, preparing a good breakfast for the menfolk to tuck into once the essentials were accomplished. Ramsey thought on his middle daughter. The girl was fair. Such a pretty little thing. She had a lighter complexion than either Delphi or Filia had. And her hair, down to her waist was a beautiful shade of golden brown. When she was younger, just a tadpole of a thing, her brown eyes had started to show the glinting light of the sun, not the deep midnight of her Ma. And now, darned if the little peepers weren't a mossy shade of green. Ramsey's own grandmother had had green eyes. It made him smile to think that this daughter carried some mark of the Youngblood line in her beauty.

But the poor thing was grown too fast. It was a matter of course, losing her Ma as she had, and then Filia off and married.

It weighed on Ramsey's heart. Boys. Well boys, he understood. But with no woman in the house, he pondered sending Bonnie off to live with Neosha and Atsadi. At least her grandmother could teach her how to be a wife and mother, even if it was too late to give her a real childhood. And her Little Hawk grandparents were aging. Was it fair to send her there? Would she fare better with Filia, like Seth was doing? But was that fair to anyone? Filia and Happy should be starting their own family, not raising his. What about one of her aunts? Nesa and Ats were already being looked after by Uncle David and Aunt Miriam. Nothing was fair. His pappy always said, God doesn't promise us life will always be happy, but He does promise us that He will be our strength. Ramsey stopped and closed his eyes. He was a simple man. And his prayer was simple.

God guide me. Help me raise Delphi's girl right.

There had been so much hard going in the lives of these women. Lord, Ramsey knew that and had been there to see the sorrow. It had broken Jetty, but he had seen Delphi grow stronger for the pain. Generational curses. The bible was full of them. Ramsey knew. He and Delphi had prayed about it late at night together. This family could be torn, or it could be strengthened. And Little Mama had always only seen one option. She always stitched things back together.

He stood there a bit longer, loving and missing his wife. Wishing he had the heart left to weep a little more. And then, his heart heard an answer. Perhaps God would send someone to help mend things. Ramsey just had to mend and open his heart. It would be hard. Annie. Delphi.

He sighed and wiped a calloused hand over his weary eyes. Another prayer. Simple, yet so heartfelt.

Lord, Father, bring me strength that I be not torn. For I promised there was no other choice.

Iko Neosha and Agiduda Atsadi were getting older. Their grand-children revered them, as was the way between generations. Ancestors were an important part of self-identity to most Native people. Sweet Filia was a cherished visitor for her elders. As their first grandchild, she had a keen interest in the stories and practices that both of her origin tribes held dear. It was important to pass both the Cherokee and Osage tribal ways down to the younger ones. Their people must not die out.

Now Bonnie had a preemptive soft spot in their hearts. The young girl was surrounded by boys since Filia had left home and married. Bonnie's responsibilities were heavy. She cooked and cleaned and generally looked after the Youngblood menfolk. But even more so, Neosha-as the grandmother-felt the need to pass just as much on to Bonnie as she had to Filia. These two branches of the spreading family tree needed strong female medicine to grow properly.

As for Bonnie herself, she was delighted to be the focus of her grandmother's attention. Granny Neosha, or Iko, as she had been taught to call the older woman, was teaching her the Osage language and healing. She learned about the plants and trees that kept the family well. She knew how to use the sage and sing the prayers that kept them safe. Iko Neosha also shared some of the Cherokee ways she had learned that came down on Astadi's side. Agiduda meant revered grandfather. And Bonnie loved the smile she got every time she greeted her grandfather this way. Though it was not generally something girls spent time on, she was learning some basic tool making skills from Agiduda. She could knap a fine point, but she could easily see that the grinding base and stone Iko had given her was of much more practical use.

Her brothers were treating her with respect. Finally. That had been a battle. Not even her father's stern reprimands had altered their behavior. But then, after a fishing trip with Atsadi, the boys had come to her solemnly, one by one, and thanked her for her commitment and service to their home. Now she felt special, the way Little Mama and Filia had been special to the family in their task of keeping the home. She missed Mama and Filia both, but she couldn't help but feel closer to them as she went about her day. She was treading the same path they had walked before her.

Now Papa, he was another matter. Always quiet, he said almost nothing beyond his please and thank you. He led the family in prayer at meals. And he always had a word with the Pastor or the grown men in the family. But his eyes were sad, and his heart was heavy. After consulting Iko Neosha, Bonnie had discreetly placed a good size piece of quartz under his bed frame. And she had smudged and used salt and rosemary in the room her father and mother had shared. She lifted him up to Creator and hoped that these things would bring him peace. She wanted that with all her heart. She could not imagine any more sorrow or great change in her life than she had already faced. She simply wanted to see that everyone was happy.

9

The Baileys went to the church that Sunday morning, expecting to see their family. Filia had baked pies in the hotel kitchen. They were wrapped in flannel and tucked safely under the wagon seat for the dinner they would all enjoy that afternoon.

But when they entered the church house, Atsadi and Neosha were not there. They did not arrive late and when the service was over, the clan gathered outside. David and Ox had helped their father cull the chicken flock on Friday afternoon. No one had visited on Saturday, but no one had thought anything amiss, either. There was a slight shared feeling that perhaps the elders were ill, so everyone loaded up and headed to the homestead as planned.

As the families arrived at the small clapboard farmhouse, they saw Neosha on the porch. She was seated on the porch floor, cross legged with an earthenware bowl in her lap. There were green beans in the bowl and a poke beside her right knee. She had obviously been snapping beans, but now her hands rested still, in her lap. Her eyes were closed.

Filia approached her slowly and sat down, cross legged, directly in front of her granny.

"Iko? Are you well? Where is Agiduda?"

The other women had gathered on the porch and squatted around the matriarch. Neosha slowly opened her eyes,

"My beloved did not return from the field for supper yesterday evening."

The women glanced around at one another. Then Pat placed a reassuring hand on her mother in law's shoulder. She spoke in a soft, comforting tone,

"Mother, have you been here ever since then?"

Neosha's voice was steady and resolved. Her words seemed to carry the weight of the world, but her lined face was at peace,

"Yesterday evening, it began to grow dim and yet Atsadi had not returned from chores. I washed my hands and laid aside my apron. Then I stepped out to the backyard to watch for him across the fields. I did not see him. So, I called for him. The world grew silent. It is then that I heard the ancestors. A warmth wrapped around me. Atsadi was here, but not. I could hear him sing with the old ones. I went about my work and started on the beans. I have waited here since, hoping for his voice so I would know my next steps. But I have not heard him again. Only the owl…last night, Friday night, and the eve before that."

David went into the kitchen and appeared once again. He carried Atsadi's flask. Neosha drank first, and then the whiskey was passed about among the men. As Filia and the ladies gathered Neosha up and moved her to the kitchen, the men all headed across the fields to retrieve the body. Neosha ate just a bit, and when everyone returned, Ox entered the kitchen.

"His heart. He was laid easily on the ground behind the plow hitched to that big old draft horse. Butter must have watched vigil all night. Like you, on the porch."

Neosha lifted her chin and looked into her son's eyes. She simply nodded and patted him on the shoulder.

The men moved stoically to the barn where Atsadi was laid out. There was a coffin to build and dirt work to be done. The word would need to be given to the community. The women would see to a meal and a shroud. Plans and efforts would take up the next three days. Yet the heaviest things that lay before them were the memories.

The days that followed were hard. It was a small comfort that Atsadi was in heaven with Delphi and Jetty and those of his grandchildren who did not survive infancy. Ophelia and Bonnie fussed over Neosha. She was no spring chicken herself and her bones grew tired and gave her trouble on colder days.

Ramsey had been working the crops, trying to keep up both farms with the help of his sons and in-laws. He had stopped for a moment to take a swig from his water skin and wipe his brow. It was then that he saw Neosha coming across the field at a good pace. He waved and then sat to wait. When she reached him, she lowered herself to the ground and looked at him hard.

"Son, I've a thought, and it's you who must decide, but it makes good sense and I see no better way."

Ramsey nodded and his smile encouraged the old lady to go on,

"Bonnie has been a concern to us both, since Delphi passed. With Ophelia in town, wee Bonnie is adrift amidst the fellows, since Nesa is still so little. Now I know you must have thought about a new mam for them all. And no one would fault you that. But I sure don't see you getting in a rush about it, nor doing anything to make it come about."

Ramsey looked up at the early afternoon sky,

"Bonnie needs a woman. That is certain. And she also needs unburdened a bit so she can be a child. But you are right, I think I will not love again. Losing Annie was rough. But putting Delphi in the ground has broken my heart in a way that a man cannot put back together. And no lady is better than one I could not love…. it's a pickle."

Neosha leaned in close and took Ramsey's arm,

"Son, my house is empty. For sure, company is regular, but the nights are dark and quiet. I would take her. She has much to learn, and I have much to teach. We would be company for one another, and I will make sure she does not grow up too fast. For my part, well, I have selfish reasons. I miss my girls."

Ramsey sat up straighter and smiled. Yes, this would do. And as far as mending and such, the women's work, Neosha and Bonnie could help he and the boys. In return, the men could take over Atsadi's fields and chores. This would suit just fine. God had answered Ramsey's prayers.

They were sure Bonnie would be most pleased. She spent as much time there with her Iko as possible. She could grow up kind and wise with Neosha's guidance so that she would make a suitable wife and mother one day. All the while, she would be easing Neosha's loneliness and helping as the woman grew older. They made plans to meet at the Youngblood house for supper and break the news to Bonnie there.

Bonnie, Neosha, Ophelia, and Maggie sat in the parlor at the hotel. Their eyes closed; heads bowed. Granny Neosha said the Lord's prayer, and they all tucked into a late lunch. Filia had made fancy finger chicken salad sandwiches. It was a family favorite, especially among the ladies. Neosha recited the story about how Ramsey and Delphi had eaten them right there in the hotel while on their honeymoon. She described the way Delphi had ciphered out the ingredients so she could make the sandwiches at home on her own. And the recipe had passed throughout the family. It made them all smile.

Neosha looked well. Having Bonnie with her at the Little Hawk homestead was working magic for everyone. Bonnie was brimming over with information she was learning, and Iko Neosha was generous with her encouragement.

For her part, Maggie had plenty to share. Her children, George and little Anna were energetic children. They got along well together but had some mischief about them. Today, Maggie shared the tale of how they had captured frogs from the pond and were patiently watching for tadpoles to appear in a bucket. Every morning, Anna woke up crowing,

"Today's the day!"

Then George would call her a ninny and they would roll about the floor as though a well-placed slap might make the frog eggs hatch faster.

All four of the ladies had taken to fits of laughter over the story and were trying to catch their breath. Once calm again, Filia spoke,

"I love having you here whenever we can see each other. But today is special for a different reason. I have something I have been longing to tell, and now I believe I have sat on it long enough and the cat should be let out of the bag...."

Neosha went stock still and quiet. She had a broad smile on her face and her eyes were closed. Maggie plucked at Filia's sleeve impatiently as Bonnie bounced in her chair,

"Oh, do tell. Please please? I cannot abide the waiting of a surprise."

Neosha opened her eyes and met Filia's gaze with a small nod. The smiles exchanged were contagious, so Filia simply blurted it out.

"I am with child! The babe has quickened. The doctor and my math tell four months hence we shall have a little one!"

Like a shot, Maggie was out of her chair and had her arms flung round her sister in law's shoulders. Bonnie kept on with the bouncing and clapped her hands. Neosha reached forth and gave her oldest granddaughter's hand a squeeze. Then she looked knowingly at Filia,

"Perfect timing my Sweet. Little Nohpazi is toddling and almost out of his clouts." She counted out the months on her fingers.

"September," Neosha said, "very wise. The hotel will be slow that time of year. Crops will be coming in and we can take turns coming to stay with you and help here as you near your time. Oh child, how happy you make me. I will see my great granddaughter."

Filia looked at her skeptically,

"Daughter? How can you know?"

"Your hair is thickening, and I notice you have little appetite. These are telling signs. But we will know with more certainty once you show, and we see how the little one sits."

Filia was delighted. Nohpazi filled her heart. He was a kind and loving little boy. He followed Happy everywhere he went. Now a daughter would balance things nicely and she would have her own little shadow as well. Filia made the ladies promise to keep their tongues until Sunday after church. Then Happy could tell everyone at lunch.

There would be gowns and blankets to sew and knit. Ribbons and bows to make. The cradle would be put to use once more. Nohpazi had been sleeping in a trundle for some time now, big boy that he was. Filia hoped with all her heart it was indeed a girl. Sons would come later, but she could not wait to hold this child in her arms. September could not come soon enough.

The hot summer passed and with each day, Filia's belly grew bigger. She was carrying high. And she could not get enough of sweets. Happy brought her a bag of barley sugars from the mercantile next door every few days. Neosha assured them that this did indeed indicate a girl child. Dear Agnes, was full of prognostications herself.

One afternoon when business was slow, Agnes stealthily shut the parlor doors and bid Filia lay flat on her back of the Turkish carpet. She begged off the wedding ring Happy had given to Filia and tied it with a piece of ribbon that she had soaked in rainwater and left to dry under a full moon.

"Now," Agnes said, "close your eyes and clear your mind."

She held the ring by the ribbon and dangled it over Filia's rounded middle.

"Oh yes! Yay, yay, yay!" Agnes shouted.

Filia sat up with wide eyes.

"What on earth, Agnes Keys Smith!? Why the ruckus?"

Agnes answered her in a rush of emotion and a huge smile,

"It swung immediately into a perfect circle. That's a girl for sure. And she's right under your rib cage. And the sweets. A girl for sure. But we can try just one or two more things. Here, let's go into the kitchen and you eat a clove of garlic. If your breath doesn't stink after, it is a girl for sure!"

Filia covered her giggle with a demure hand. She shook her head in fits of laughter.

Then Agnes grew very serious. She put a hand on Filia's elbow and pulled her to the other side of the parlor, as far from the door as possible. She cast her eyes about furtively and dipping her head, she whispered something so low, Filia could not understand her.

Filia cocked an eyebrow and told her to speak up.

Agnes blushed from her hairline all the way to her bodice.

"Oh, all right, but I only ask in the name of science" she dropped her voice again' "what position did you.....ah.... that is.....when the child was conceived, who was....."

"Agnes!" Filia burst out, "Why, I never!"

Agnes was cherry red by now.

"Well," she said, "it matters not. We shall see in a matter of weeks. But I am still betting on a girl. 'Specially if you were…"

"That's enough!" Filia scolded.

And both young women collapsed into giggles.

The late summer morning was already unbearable. The humidity, even at this predawn moment, was like the runoff of some sulfur spring venting straight up from hades.

Filia was out on the raised sidewalk in front of the Hotel. She was sweeping away all the dust and tobacco juice that tended to appear in miraculous abundance overnight for such a quiet sundown town. Now and ever more frequently, she put a hand to her lower back and straightened up. Sometimes stretching to her full height would alleviate the pressure this babe seemed to be putting on her spine. Her bump was front and center, even if she mostly felt her child moving against her ribs and lower back.

She took those lumps along with the joys of the tiny kicks and the movement in response to her voice, and especially Happy's singing. She had witnessed the pregnancies and losses of her mother and her sisters in law. And that equated to quite a bit of exposure. This had served her well going through this first pregnancy. She had little Nohpazi, and in her heart he was every bit her son. But this baby would be the first born from her body.

Granny Neosha was also proving indispensable through her waiting time. As Filia got bigger, Neosha came to town more often. Up until now, Filia and Happy were accustomed to going out to the Little Hawk/Youngblood farm to visit. It was a trip they could make blindfolded as that is where they found their family, and just down the road was their cherished Denver Church prayer house. But now, in the heat with this tiny bare-knuckle fighter -as Happy named it -growing rapidly every day, Neosha and her sisters and in-laws obliged them by coming to the Hotel quite frequently. Someone seemed to pop in every day. And they were always gently steering Filia to a chair and ottoman, just to "rest a minute." The tight knit family fell into their familiar pattern of helping one another out and tasking without prompting. They knew each other. And they knew Filia would have to be forced to cease her whirlwind productivity and simply slowdown in these last days of her condition.

Filia had no more gone into the kitchen pantry and changed her apron for a fresh one when it happened. She was startled at first, but immediately identified the puddle at her feet as the baby's waters. The gush was quickly followed with a sharp cutting pain in her low back that nearly pitched her forward and onto her knees. Happy was up and right out in the back plot thankfully. She raised her voice and called to him. He had been on pins and needles ever since the doctor confirmed they were going to be parents. Accordingly, his head shot round the back-door frame within seconds of his wife's call.

What he found was a surprisingly silent Filia with a very round open mouth, trying to spy her own feet and the puddle that dampened them. With a joyful outburst, Happy shouted,

"Praise the Lord, here comes my baby! Seth! Seth!! Boot up and get down here!"

Seth raced bleary eyed down the stairs and stopped stock still in front of his sister. Happy let out a hardy laugh when he saw that the faces of his wife and her sibling matched almost identically.

"OK, Seth, like we talked. Ride Lily, she's faster. Go straight to Doc's and send him here. Then go up on Sparks Road and knock on Agnes Smith's door. She already agreed to be with Filia in her travail. They will remember, but also remind them that her husband Zeke is to ride out to Neosha and see that she comes to town as well."

Seth did not miss a beat as he grabbed an apple and a biscuit off the kitchen table and raced to the horse shed. It never crossed his mind to saddle or bridle Lily. He just planted himself on her, barebacked, and pressed his left knee against her shoulder, turning out of the shelter and into the back lot. He'd learned to ride from his Uncle David. There was a notable difference in the way Seth's People and other folks communicated with their animals. And Seth was glad of it today, as this was a swift and important mission and he had not needed to waste any time preparing the mare to work with him. They were one now as they tore toward Doc's clapboard house over on Center Street.

Meanwhile, at the Hotel, Happy had convinced Filia to stop dropping tea towels and trying to bend over and clean up the waters by quickly sweeping her up into both arms and carrying her up the floors to their private living quarters. Everything was ready and had been for weeks. The beautiful handmade cradle that Atsadi had carved before Filia's OWN birth was standing in the corner. For a swift second, she closed her eyes and thought of little Esther Patience who had laid there still and lifeless while their mother Delphi and labored over her- Filia- the unexpected bonus twin. It was almost like Delphi, Atsadi, and Esther were all a part of this day, watching over her with all of the ancestors. She began to sing the birthing song that her mother and grandmother had taught her. She knew it would all be well, and that the doctor was on his way, but in this moment, it was Neosha she longed for. And soon, her granny would be there by her side just like Happy, holding her hand.

The pangs came hard and fast. It was no surprise that Filia felt an undeniable urge to push. But where was the doctor? And Agnes? Both Filia and Happy expected Neosha's arrival to take some time, with her farm being some distance from town. But honestly! The doctor was only up the hill and two roads over.

Try as he might, Happy could not keep Filia in the bed. She kept a strong hold on the wooden corner post at the foot. She swayed, switching her weight from one foot to the other. She crooned her birthing song without ceasing unless the contraction was strong. Then she would pause her tune only long enough to silently blow out her breath until the pressure eased. She would immediately go back to her song, as if she had never stopped,

"We are stars that fall from night sky

Peace, Baby, Peace.

Raven and Red Elk are gathered nearby

Peace, Baby, Peace.

Mother's a warrior and you will be so,

Peace, Baby, Peace.

Creator has given me as your home,

Peace, Baby, Peace."

Still no doctor, no Agnes, and no Neosha, Happy was beginning to gather his steam. Filia was calm but she was obviously in pain. The pauses in her song were coming more and more frequently. Happy had just suggested she lay on the bed for the hundredth time and was met by a silent and serious look his direction, when they heard the bell on the front door. Happy was relieved beyond measure.

"Up here!" he called, knowing the visitor must be one of the expected folks that Seth had alerted.

"Happy Bailey," Filia said through gritted teeth," best come here and sit on the floor behind me..."

Filia's voice was calm yet firm. Happy blinked twice and quickly moved to sit where she asked, his knees folded and directly behind her heels. Footsteps could be heard on the first landing. But Happy and Filia were now deeply involved in a world of their own. The time was now.

"Now Happy, love, please reach up and feel my hand. It is resting on our child's head and keeping her from dropping to the floor. Please hold her head and neck with both hands so I can push. She is almost with us."

Happy reached up under Filia's night gown. There was a huge lump in his throat. His mother had birthed 16 children in her time. There were 13 living including himself. But NEVER before had he been in the room during travail. When his father was alive, Happy would join him outside and talk with him about anything to drown out the noise and din of the birth. But this was his baby, and he did not hesitate to follow Filia's instructions. Now and always, they were of perfect accord.

First, he felt the back of his wife's hand. Indeed, he could feel that it cupped a wee head full of hair. The minute his hands were in place, securing their precious child, Filia moved her hand. She grabbed back hold of the bed post and with knees bent, anxiously awaited the next contraction. As she blew out her air and pushed down as mightily as she could, she heard her mother Delphi's voice,

"Peace, Baby, Peace."

There was a quick rush of fluid, and Happy pulled the tiny bundle from beneath Filia's nightgown. Filia sunk to her knees beside him, and they looked into the face of their child. They did not notice until then that Agnes, Neosha, and Doc were standing in the door frame.

Everyone took quick action. Happy and Doc got Filia and the baby up onto the bed. As soon as the cord was cut, Neosha and Agnes took the baby and began to clean her up. Happy gently kissed the top of Filia's head and held her hand as the doctor took care of the necessary matters. Filia was well, fine, even. For she could hear the lusty cries of her baby.

Once Granny Neosha deemed the mite clean and presentable, she handed her great granddaughter to the parents. She was wrapped in the same beautiful blanked that had swaddled Filia years ago. Happy and Filia looked down at the beautiful face.

Their daughter wasn't much lighter than Nohpazi, but her hair was a very deep mahogany red. She had much more hair than the usual newborn, and it lay in wet ringlets against her tiny head. When she opened her wide blinking eyes, they were a startling green! Filia gasped in delight and then laughed out loud. She had a little curly red headed green eyed Osage baby. Everyone in the room agreed that they had never seen the like. But MY, was she not a beautiful little thing?

"She must have a name, granddaughter," Neosha said.

Filia looked up and nodded. There was an enormous smile on her face,

"Catie, for Happy's mother. It shows her heritage. And Lynn. For that was Aunt Jettimae's middle name. And ancestors are important. I think my own mother would agree. Catie Lynn."

Everyone was grinning when the doctor spoke up,

"For the birth certificate, then: Catie Lynn."

Kathy nuzzled her face into her mama's breast and began to nurse.

10

ife had never been dull or common feeling. But now, with two small children, a hotel to run, a younger brother to guide, and a husband to fill her heart, Filia's days were a whirlwind. And, being the true spawn of her mother, grandmother, and great grandmother before them, she positively bloomed into her roles.

Family, or really, the tribe, had been the axis on which her whole reality focused. This was the way of her people. She knew that when Creator was drafting His great design, each piece was stitched together with purpose. Filia had learned the Osage creation story about the Sun, Moon, Stars, Raven, and Red Elk as a toddler. It was repeated again and again to her throughout her childhood. And later, she had told the same tale to Ats and Nesa, Bonnie, and her younger brothers. Even now, she crooned the history to Nohpazi and Little Catie at nap times.

But she had also grown up in her father's house, and she was taken faithfully to the Denver Community Church every single Sunday she could remember. There, Creator was called God. And the Bible and song books that told the creation tale were different. There were many, many kinds of people created so it did not seem confusing for her that there were different origins for those tribes. The Church Bible said that the clay Earth was the mother of Man. And that Creator God was the father, using his breath to create life. When He breathed into Adam, He left a piece of Himself inside. This was the third part of the trinity they sang about. Father, Son, and Spirit. There must be a piece of Creator left in everything He made. This was where Filia's parents' beliefs intertwined. So, it was of no great matter to her to fit these two histories together for her children and see no contradiction. Her Grandfather had told of relatives that believed the entire world rested on the back of a great terrapin. This knowledge was older than the written word. And Filia was not in the business of elevating herself to question such things.

She was delivering a much more simplified explanation of these elements to the children when it happened. Sweet, quiet Nohpazi was sitting on the rug in the hotel parlor listening and lining up his wooden horses. Catie was nursing contentedly under a modest shawl. She had grown into a bubbly, russet, round doll. She cooed and smiled and carried on conversations with everyone. Though only Catie knew what she was actually saying, it drew everyone's adoration.

Suddenly, Filia felt her daughter go very rigid. Simultaneously, her latch slacked, and she stopped sucking. Filia frantically flung off the covering and lifted her daughter upright. Her lids were open, but the left eye was rolled so far back, only the white showed. The baby's right eye canted drastically outward as though she was trying to see over her own shoulder. Then Catie's tiny back arched and her limbs and head began to jerk in rapid fierce spasms. Filia had not a thought in her head. She only acted.

"Noha, stay right here. Line your horses up and watch them close. Be a very VERY good little man and DO NOT LEAVE THIS ROOM."

Then she grasped Catie to her chest and ran out the front door of the Hotel lobby onto the sidewalk. She whipped her head left to right. There were train passengers, men, and women walking around entering and exiting the buildings that lined Main Street. There. Directly across the road she saw Widow Dunfield. Constance Dunfield was almost as old as Granny Neosha. She had 7 grown children and at least a dozen grands and some greats. In the absence of Neosha or the doctor, Widow Dunfield would stand a better chance of knowing anything and everything about babies than any other citizen in view.

As Filia called out to her, Catie continued to thrash steadily and upon inspection, her mouth was slack and her whole cheek wet with saliva. Mrs. Dunfield picked her way quickly through the traffic of main street and half ran up to the raised sidewalk where both mother and precious child were now slumped to the stones. The two women were eye level and now Filia was shaking almost as much as Catie.

"Hush, child. Hand her to me, "directed the widow.

It was then that Filia realized she had been screaming the entire time. She did as she was told and gently passed her baby to the older lady. Filia's face was wet with tears. Her eyes were wide with terror, and her mind was racing. But as she watched, she understood immediately what it was that the widow was doing. She had tilted Catie forward, facing downwards and had slipped her finger into the child's toothless mouth between her tongue and the roof. So, she wouldn't swallow it and choke.

Doctor Martin had been very gentle and patient. Happy was home there with her by the time they heard what Doc had to say. Most children, if not all, could be expected to have at least one spell in infancy. He had called it a febrile fit. It had to do with fever and the way the child's body reacted. Filia was not pacified. Little Catie had not felt hot. She had not been sickly before she took the breast that afternoon. If anything, she was more jolly than usual. Still, Doc advised that Aspirin could be used. Filia was very familiar with meadow sweet and willow bark. They were tried and true remedies for fever and pain, but she still went to the druggist. There had been much ado in the past few years about the wonders of that soft white powder. In her heart she knew it was the same kind of medicine. She could have prepared her own remedy as Neosha had taught her. But the baby could ingest the finely ground aspirin much easier, and it would be ready on hand. She would take no chances with her children. She prayed silently to Creator that she would never need to use the drug and that Catie would never have a fit again.

She and Happy loaded up the children and drove out to Denver for church on Sunday. The sermon was inspiring and once again, Filia prayed fervently for the health of BOTH of her children. Afterwards they spread blankets under the trees by the burying grounds. The entire extended family loved these Homecoming fellowship Sundays. Everyone could eat and talk together. They watched the toddlers and older children play and caught up on the news of one another. Sundays at the farm were wonderful too. But Homecoming Sundays allowed for a nice chat with neighbors, friends, and more distant relations.

Ophelia had taken a cool shady spot against the trunk of an oak tree. She held a sleeping Catie. It was very hard not to fuss and worry over the infant all the time. But she would not give way to her fear and make her daughter into a fussbudget or take away her natural confidence and wonder. With her was her sister-in-law Maggie. She loved Maggie special, as it was she who had introduced Happy that day on a similar picnic years before. Maggie and Happy were cousins, and they shared the same customs and history of the Irish. It was always a pleasant day when she could share it with Maggie. Neosha and Bonnie joined them as well. Bonnie was not quite 11 but she seemed so much older. Filia was proud of her little sister. She had become matriarchal, just as Filia had done as their mother weakened and grew ill before she passed. Before long, though, Bonnie jumped up and raced over to her cousins to play. As she should.

It was then that Filia shared with Maggie and Iko Neosha the nightmare of Catie's spasms. Maggie reached over and patted both mother and baby daughter sweetly. Neosha was very quiet. After a time, she began to speak,

"I have heard of these fits before. And I speak no ill of our good doctor. But, child, he is calling something a fever, which it is not. I have not passed a thought over this in years, but I will share a story with you now.

Many many years ago, when Atsadi and I were still east and before we came to this farm, we lived near his family. Your grandfather does not...did not...speak much about his family or his Cherokee people after we came to Arkansas. This is because, though we honor our old ones, revere our ancestors, and remember the ways, we do not revisit sorrow when it can be helped. Atsadi had an older brother and a younger sister. Neither of them lived to grow and marry. His brother Standing Bear was found dead when he was 8 years old. He had choked and there had been no one to see or help. Atsadi never spoke of his sister, as she was not even walking when she died. Yet the family say they had something called the Falling Sickness. Mind you, the little I know came through in bits and pieces of conversation with my mother-in-law. She was a quiet sad woman. She mourned when Atsadi and I married as if she had seen all three of her children put in the earth. But she did love us. And she doted on Ox and David as babies before we came west. This is why I tell you about your grandfather's family:

All her children except Atsadi 'fitted' as you describe from a very early age. She treated them with willow bark, meadow sweet, zinc and camphor. You see, his siblings did not have fevers when they suffered. And it started much like you tell. Fits and spasms. Almost like fainting but with rapid movements instead of stillness. They would bite their tongues and cheeks. They would choke on their own spit or lose their food from their stomachs. They would be like this for minutes and then it would cease. Sleep after could last for hours or days...Filia, dear child, be vigilant. As they grew, became more mobile, these spirits would come on with no warning. We have felt so blessed that none of our children or grandchildren suffered this illness. But if Catie does have this Falling Sickness, we are better for our knowledge of it and the chance to be prepared."

Neosha reached out and took beautiful dozing Catie from her mother's arms. Ophelia wiped the tears that had long since wet her face and that of her daughter. Maggie scooted closer and held Filia tight.

Neosha shushed Filia while she rocked the baby,

"Come to the farm on Tuesday. I will have the physic ready for you. And there will always be some on hand."

Catie was walking now, and Filia's hands were constantly full. The little girl had had a handful of more seizures, but each day she was given a sweet cup of milky tea made out of moon water with the precious powders mixed in. Filia was convinced that the fits were fewer and farther between, even less severe for the regimen. But Catie still had times where she would grow stiff, and her limbs would contort. It was hard to watch.

Neosha, Filia and Bonnie worked together to collect the ingredients and make sure that the little pouch Filia carried in her apron pocket was always full. They had added different amounts of additional plants to the willow bark and meadowsweet mixture, including lavender. It seemed to work much better than the aspirin and sodium bromate that Doctor Martin swore by. The few times that Cathy had spasmed, Filia had taken a fingerful of powder and reached inside the little child's clenched jaws to rub the physic on the baby's cheek. It seemed to work. Still, when she spoke, Catie's words came slow, and she seemed to have a lazy eye. Filia also spent a lot of time in prayer.

Agnes was still a dear friend. She had two sweet little girls just older and then younger than Catie. They had the same dark curls as their mother and got along well with Catie. On this day, the two women sat in the back doorway of the hotel and watched Noha, and the three little girls chase the chickens about in the yard. They each had a bowl in their lap and worked from a common sack, shelling peas. Agnes noted that Filia had grown quiet. She seemed lost in her thoughts.

"Filia, are you alright? You have something on your mind."

Filia sighed deeply and stretched, placing both hands on her lower back.

"I've another baby started. And I worry about the time and energy, what with Catie."

Agnes said nothing but continued to shell peas. She had been friends with Filia long enough to know that if Ophelia was ready to talk, she would.

"Happy wants a boy. So, I stopped drinking my tea. It seemed a fine idea at the time, and Catie is doing so much better. But I never remember feeling this tired before, and the baby's not even here yet."

Agnes reached over and placed her hand on Filia's arm,

"How far gone?"

"I'm thinking four months. I should feel him soon. I find it almost impossible to get through the day without joining Catie in her nap. Noha rarely naps well anymore, but he is content to play quietly while we doze," Filia confided.

She and Agnes began reminiscing about their earlier pregnancies and their postpartum memories of sweet-smelling newborns. After the conversation, Filia felt considerably lighter. She and Agnes laughed together as they watched their little girls tackle and tickle Noha.

The seasons turned and it was fall again. Filia was sweeping the raised sidewalk in front of the Bailey's Hotel. Five-year-old Nohpazi sat just inside the open doorway reading the newspaper out loud to his mother. He was knee deep in an editorial submission about the Carroll County horse auction that was coming up. Sweet Catie was drawing finger pictures in the dirt that her mother had not yet swept away. The child was talking softly to herself as her dark red curls blew in the breeze. She had just celebrated her third birthday and her health was good. Her gaze had straightened and the concern that she might be wall eyed had passed. She would probably always be a quiet, careful child. It was only to be expected after the frightening spells. But both Filia and Happy worked hard to make sure she had an active and normal childhood.

"Hello, my sweets!" Happy called out in greeting as he and Seth bounded up the stairs from the street to the Hotel front.

"Are we all working together and having a nice time?"

Catie squealed a greeting and held up her arms to be lifted as Nohpazi practically climbed Happy in excitement. Noha was sputtering a million words a minute as he tried to tell Happy about the auction.

Seth leaned against the wall and played with a handkerchief, idly. He was doing well, and the rockworks and he was courting. Filia smiled at him proudly. Surely this lacy handkerchief was a token from a sweetheart. Set caught Filia's eye and winked at her slyly, then bounded into the Hotel and up the steps to his room high in the attic.

Her husband now had their sweet girl on his hip, and Noha on his shoulders. He leaned in to give Filia a quick peck. When he spoke again, his eyes were bright and full of love, "

"How are you my love? And how is our peanut?" His glance slid to her growing stomach.

Filia was standing with the broom in one hand and her other hand resting underneath her belly, supporting it.

"Another tap dancer, Happy. He will not let me sit or lay or stand for anytime at all, but what he demands a change!" she smiled tiredly," He's feisty."

Happy asked if there had been any pains yet. She told him that she knew her body was getting ready but felt like they had at least a few weeks left. If her calculations were correct, this son would join them before Thanksgiving.

Filia silently slipped out from beneath the quilt, stood and stretched. She made sure not to wake her husband. The pains had started after they went to bed, before the moon hit its high spot in the black night. But now they were intensifying. She knew that in just a few hours, they were all due a flurry of activity, and she wanted these last quiet moments to herself.

She carefully picked her way down the stairs to the ground floor. She only had to stop twice and breathe thru the clenching pain of contractions. Now she chose the most comfortable chair in the kitchen, a rocker, to wait for her tea kettle to boil. She would make a tea of primrose, raspberry leaf and wild lettuce leaf. This would strengthen her womb and move her labor on.

She had opened the back door so she could be a part of the deep purple-black pre-dawn. She heard an owl. But only a screech owl and only once. So, she was not alarmed. Shortly she would wake Happy and Seth, sending one or the other for Neosha. But not just yet. The rooster wasn't even awake, but she could hear the snuffling exhale of one or another of the mules. They were all tucked in their stalls for the night. She knew they were warm and cozy. She could almost smell the sweet hay and leather smells that permeated the barn and filled her nose whenever she was close to the animals.

Another pain. Sharper this time. She breathed through and then rose and prepared her tea. She did not notice the trickle that ran down her leg. Cup in hand she turned to climb the stairs back up to bed with her husband. Suddenly, another sharp pain, but this was a tearing pain. She screamed as the trickle turned to a rush. This was not her waters, this was blood.

11

He was here. The long-wanted son of Dewey and Ophelia Bailey was a bouncing, wailing 13-pound beautiful baby. He was the largest child Dr. Martin could remember delivering. The boy had his mother's dark skin, raven hair, and midnight eyes. But his father was well represented in the tight pin curls that decorated his precious head. His arrival, however, was marred by sadness and concern along with the natural joy.

The infant had been turned backwards and his position could not be corrected. So, he had been born breech. Filia had fought valiantly and pushed and pushed for hours until she passed out. Doctor Martin had needed to use forceps. Filia was wounded and bruised, but then another complication presented itself immediately. Instead of passing the placenta, her entire womb was expelled. She prolapsed and there was nothing Dr. Martin could do. He saved Filia's life, but she lost her ability to bear any more children. Just like her mother.

Filia was exhausted and on the brink of sleep. Happy sat gingerly on the edge of the bed holding their boy.

"He must have a name, my girl. You've worked so hard. What shall we call him?"

Filia sighed and thought, then a grin split her face.

"Josiah Youngblood Bailey. After my Papa's daddy. I only met him a handful of times, but, oh Happy, what a magnificent man he was. You know, he fought in the Civil War. For the Yankees, even. He didn't hold with oppression. He was a General, such a presence! The stories he told!"

Happy closed his eyes, he was ruminating in the most serious manner. Then he swallowed and spoke,

"Allow me the tiniest change, my dear: General Josiah Youngblood Bailey. We'll call him 'General.'"

Filia's eyes opened wide. She repeated the name out loud and laughed.

"I love it, I truly do. Noha, Catie and General. Our family is full."

Happy leaned forward, placed General against his wife's breast and kissed her on the forehead.

After her birthing ordeal, Filia had a hard time with it. She knew she was going to have to accept some help. Seth and Happy managed to feed and dress Catie and Noha, but then they were both off to work- Seth to the Rock Works and Happy on one thing or another. Agnes came and sat midday and helped with lunch, but she was now heavily pregnant herself and while she could herd the children, she did not need to be lifting and helping Filia. Yet Filia still required quite a bit of assistance and was mostly bed ridden.

There was nothing for it. Neosha and Bonnie would have to come to the Hotel to stay for a while. Neosha had suggested when she came to sit with Filia after church on Sunday. Then she had gone home for a few days to gather what she needed and to make arrangements for the Youngblood and Little Hawk men to keep her farm up. After that, she and Bonnie headed into town.

Bonnie was almost 15 now and so very very beautiful. She was much fairer than most of her siblings. She had soft brown hair and liquid bright eyes. She had a grace and solemnity about her that comes only from having a soul that is wise beyond its years. It would not be long before she was interested enough to court, but she had no beau to speak of. When she moved, it was without sound. Almost as though she was part of the atmosphere. She could stand or sit quietly for hours just observing her surroundings while almost disappearing into them at the same time. In this way, she was very much like her mother Delphi had been.

When Iko Neosha's wagon pulled up into the yard behind the Hotel, Happy was there to help them down. It was lunchtime, and Seth was also on hand, during break time at the Rock Works to help carry their parcels and baggage in. Agnes had been a priceless friend and tidied the double room up in the attic next to Seth's room for Neosha and Bonnie to share. They did not want to be separated after sharing the same room at the farm. In a half hours' time, Bonnie had hung up the bright lacy curtains and spread quilts on the bed. Neosha was in the kitchen preparing a light lunch and tea. Then they all converged in Filia's room to greet one another and eat.

It was like old times, with all the women gathered around. They doted on little General and admired Catie's curls. Noha had proudly given the prayer before the meal. He was so thoughtful and obedient. So quiet, Noha looked remarkably like his father, their beloved lost Tom. Except for those eyes. It could break the heart to look at him. They were all so thankful that Nohpazi seemed to have a serene soul and none of the brewing storm Tom had carried inside.

There was even more to be thankful for. Little Catie had not had another seizure in months. They hoped and prayed that the family ailment would not land a death blow in this case. Medicine had changed. Knowledge had been gained. And the women in the family were ever vigilant and on a heartfelt crusade to beat the little girl's affliction. No one was ready to let Catie succumb to her condition.

Soon, Filia was up and moving about again. Agnes was now the proud mother of three and came regularly to visit. Afternoons in the hotel parlor were a fine and joyous occasion. Bonnie and Iko Neosha were still there in residence. And there was almost always a lady guest or two to join them for needle work and tea in the fine parlor. They could even count on Maggie to drive in from the farm once or twice a week. Filia loved these times and was proud of the home she had made. The only thing missing was her mother, rest her soul.

Then came the day when Iko Neosha did not come down for breakfast. Filia sent Bonnie back up to the attic with simple chamomile tea and plain toast, as Bonnie reported that Iko was suffering from fearful heartburn. The pain in her chest and jaws was so severe she could not lay flat and must be propped up.

When lunch came and their grandmother was no better, Filia climbed up to the attic with fresh goats' milk and some pastilles she had fashioned from baking soda, aloe, and licorice. Ophelia's face fell when she entered the room. Iko was pale, and sweat had broken out on her brow. She was pressing her left arm tightly against her side with her right hand. Filia rushed to her side and felt Iko's brow. She was clammy. And her face was drawn into a grimace. It must be her heart.

"Sit with me, my sweet Ophelia Winsome. I'm not here for long."

Filia began to protest but Iko just put her index finger over her lips to shush her.

"Pull up a chair and hear me. There are things your mother did not get to pass on, and I will not have these things forgotten."

Filia did as she was told. As Iko Neosha began to talk, Filia leaned in to catch every work of the deep quiet voice.

"You know the story of Red Elk. Of how our People came to Earth. This is not the only way. There are many many kinds of People, so there are many Beginnings. You know the healing herbs. You know Creator, and how to pray. Your Catie will be alright because you have a reverence for our medicine. Never forget that He gave us dominion and it is a solemn responsibility to honor Creator by using His Creations.

Men need two things: a full belly and to feel clever." Iko chuckled then coughed before she went on. Her face was drawn and pale.

"As women, we also need two things. But these are very different. We need other women, and we need to keep some things secret. Like the tea. And simple beautiful things, like rose water in our hair. These secrets give us power that the world would forbid us.

Now, there is one more thing. It is a sacred secret in itself. Some have called it a curse, others a prophesy. Either way it proves true many many times in our family history. And someday you will need to pass it down along with all of the other wisdom we have gathered."

Filia helped prop Neosha up better and gave her a sip of the goat's milk and coaxed her to swallow the pastilles. Iko coughed again and her breathing had become labored.

"Granny, Iko, please let me call for Dr. Martin"

Neosha shushed her again and patted Filia's cheek.

"In a minute, Child. He cannot help me for my time is here. But I must tell you this.

Our family brings forth twins. Sacred births nearly every generation. This should be twice the joy. Twice the industry. Twice the blessing. But long ago, it was foretold that for us, twins be brought forth in cataclysm. And one day there will come a twin of this pain that will right many wrongs.

"Like Esther, like me? Iko I don't understand."

"No child, I'm not sure any of us will understand until it happens. But we are the forebearers of a paragon our People will desperately need. So, you must keep the ways. Pass on the medicine and the knowledge. We are ALL mothers to this child that is coming.

Now, I need to rest, and call the doctor if you must."

Filia leaned over and kissed her grandmother. But she was already asleep.

Neosha did not wake again. And by the next morning she was gone. She had joined Atsadi, at last. The entire town paraded out to the Little Hawk burying ground to lay her to rest. She was truly the last one of her kind in the community. But as Filia stood with Dewey and her children, paying respect and sorrowing the loss of their matriarch, her heart was full.

Deep inside, Filia was nurturing all the ideas, medicine, and secrets that her mother and her precious Iko had shared with her. This was not the end. It was simply a new beginning. And Filia would usher in this important chapter in the lives of her People. Her heart was torn, but it would never be broken. Not as long as she kept these magical women inside it.

ABOUT THE AUTHOR:

A.B. Poyner lives with her family on a farm in the Ozark Mountains of Arkansas. She is of Scottish and Native American lineage. She enjoys reading, history, music, and folk magick. She is especially fond of trees, cemeteries, and thunderstorms.